THE COMPLETE GUIDE TO STANDARD SCRIPT FORMATS

PART I - SCREENPLAYS

Compiled and written by

Hillis R. Cole, Jr.

and

Judith H. Haag

First Printing   August 1983
Eleventh Printing   April 1999
Twelfth Printing   July 2000

For information write: CMC Publishing
                          11642 Otsego Street
                          North Hollywood, California 91601

Cover Design by George E. Johannesson, Jr.

ISBN 0-929583-00-0

Dear Reader,

Our years in the script business conjure up an assortment of remembrances. CMC provided script service for the original "Laugh In" show... sometimes as many as 150 pages of one-liners and gags that carried us far into the night in our rush to get the scripts back for the next day's early morning taping. We were called Chuck's Mimeograph Company then, and shared in the excitement of many promising new shows including "The Smothers Brothers" and Tandem Production's "Sanford and Son". We also remember the very beginnings of Komack Production's "Chico and the Man" and it's meteoric rise and then fall subsequent to the tragic death of Freddie Prinze.

At times we become "insiders" privy to the future goings-on of popular shows of the moment. Our invitations to parties substantially escalated when "Mary Hartman, Mary Hartman" was taping its season, for we knew six weeks in advance her tumultuous life's fate... everything from her problems with yellow waxy build-up to her clandestine affair with a policeman. The last shows for "Let's Make a Deal" were especially exciting since we knew what was behind all the doors. (Possibly before Monty Hall did!) Our business ethics prevented us from hopping the first plane to Las Vegas to cash in on that elusive dream.

We have also watched many careers develop and unfold. By the time the first scripts for the ill-fated television series "Fay" came through, we had already marveled on previous occasions at the talents of writer Susan Harris, then working with Paul Junger Witt and Tony Thomas at Danny Thomas Productions. "300 Park Avenue, West" was a memorable and fine show she created that was never picked up. When another pilot idea of hers came to us... so zany, hilarious, frequently bizarre, and sometimes poignant, we felt it couldn't miss this time. "Soap" became one of the most popular prime time shows on the air. And still we marvel at her ability to constantly turn out excellent scripts week after week.

As script format specialists we sometimes get caught up in the games of Hollywood which necessitates that we bend the rules to fit the production company's needs. When Dino DeLaurentiis Productions first sent "King Kong" to us, the script typed out in standard format to around 140 pages -- much too long as you will find out later in this book. They called back to say, "Nice job. Can you do it again only make it much shorter?"

Through the questionable art of condensing, we re-typed the entire script with each original word intact and eliminated twenty pages from the script. (How much easier and faster this task if we'd had a word processor!)

By the time "King Kong" was finally filmed, the script along with a constant flow of revision pages had come through perhaps a dozen times. Thinking we were finally finished since the filming was completed, the script came back again like a friendly ghost. The entire script was once again typed sans camera angles along with other miscellaneous changes. This undoubtedly was the "as filmed" version incorporating all the on-the-scene ad lib material and last minute director changes that took place. This served as the legal version of the script.

While our work is mainly considered "behind the scenes" we do sometimes meet a famous well-known personality in the business. We were happy to accommodate the American Film Institute's request to use our electrical outlets for their camera cables one Sunday. A film starring Dom DeLuise, directed by Anne Bancroft, was being shot outside our offices on Sunset Boulevard. It was a surprise and a delight when Miss Bancroft wandered in searching for a place to "sit a spell" and prop her feet up.

Many scripts came through our service with neither a bang nor a whimper but some became special and even looked-forward to. "Little House On the Prairie" with its sensitive and often humorous writing, especially those episodes written by Michael Landon, were enjoyed by all of us. (Even the shooting schedules written mainly by Kent McCray frequently provided a refreshing chuckle.) And certainly it would be difficult not to get hooked into "Days of Our Lives" with its tangle of relationships and daily life's drama.

Every job has its moments. We feel that ours have been very special and we are pleased to have been able to share a few of them with you.

Hil Cole
Judy Haag

BIOGRAPHIES

JAMES F. BOYLE

B.S. Degree in Military Engineering, United States Military Academy,
    West Point (1962)
M.A. Degree in Cinema, University of Southern California
Ph.D. in Cinema-Communications, School of Cinema-TV, University of
    Southern California (1983)

Trained by the U.S. Army Signal Corps as a Motion Picture Officer
Member of DGA, graduate of the Assistant Director's Training Program
Member of IATSE Local 854 (Story Analyst Union)
Former Screenwriting Instructor, University of Southern California

HILLIS R. COLE, JR.

B.S. Degree, English, University of Illinois
M.A. Degree, Teaching, University of Illinois
Business Master, University of New Mexico
Teacher, Special Education, Centralia, Illinois
State Director, Teachers Union, New Mexico

JUDITH H. HAAG

B.S. Degree, Communications, Southern Illinois University
Teacher, High School English and Speech
Writing Consultant, Educational Film Strip Series for BFA
Former Supervisor, CMC Script Service
Former Supervisor, Barbara's Place Script Service

WITH GRATEFUL ACKNOWLEDGEMENT TO...

Lyle Law whose script format knowledge and expertise made this
manual possible.

Lyle has been lending credibility to movie and television scripts
for fifteen years. As a Format Specialist he has served in the
positions of head script typist at CMC Script Service and as
Supervisor of the Script Department at CBS.

Currently living in San Francisco, Lyle is slaving over his own
screenplay.

...and special thanks to Bert Guillen and John Cole who lent their
valuable experience, criticisms, and format expertise which aided
greatly in honing the fine details so necessary in a book such as
this!

FOREWORD

A few important concepts about creative
screenwriting which should be considered
before using this important book.

FOREWORD

Good form is more than just the correct tab settings. It is the appropriate placement of the words on the script page so the content is successfully highlighted. Just as a newspaper editor lays out the front page, so a screenplay page can be designed to be eye catching. This book contains some of the most important keys to the success of a screenplay: form and design of the page.

Having a good idea is not enough. Structuring the idea into the proper narrative, developing fine characterization and creating dialogue which serves the scene are some of the tricks in writing a screenplay. Form and design of the actual script page are often overlooked, yet they are equally important. They are unique to script writing art and not to be found in play writing or novel writing. This book is not a typing manual, it is a look at the fine line between content and form on the script page.

IN DEFENSE OF A SCREENPLAY AS AN INTERMEDIATE ART FORM

Many people scoff at the idea of defending the screenplay as a form of literature. Yet it has a sense of poetry about it. Perhaps the problem is that most people have not read enough screenplays to get a sense of the beauty of them.

Serious critics maintain that a screenplay is not an end product. They point out that the finished film is the end product and that the screenplay is only a stop-gap measure.

Admitting that a screenplay is an intermediate form of art, it may be compared to a sketch that a sculptor makes while designing a bronze statue. The actual finished product might be a life-sized statue in three dimensional form which is comparable to the three dimensional reels of emulsion in film cans which is the actual release print. Both the charcoal sketch on paper (two dimensional) and the typist's ink on paper (two dimensional script) are stop-gaps. But consider that the sculptor might be Picasso or DaVinci or Michelangelo. Then those scraps of charcoal sketches would be on display in a museum. So, too, some Academy Award winning films have their screenplays on display at museums. The day may come when a screenplay does not have to be produced and released to become considered worthy of being included in a museum's collection. At this time, Harold Pinter's script of <u>Proust</u> (an adaptation of Proust's <u>Remembrance of Things Past</u>) has not been produced, yet it has been published and is considered a fine piece of literature.

THE REASONS BEHIND SOME OF THE RULES

A typist may read this book and get a feeling for the necessary tab settings on the typewriter. Fine! However, that is only a surface function of this book. A serious beginning screenwriter will want to learn about the form, asking questions: Why is the dialogue squeezed into the middle of the page (as opposed to the theatre play which has the character name on the left margin with the dialogue strung out over the width of the page)? After reading this book, a student should be able to figure it out for himself.

A theatrical play is dependent upon the dialogue to set the off-stage exposition, the character background or the scene settings. In a play, dialogue serves a major function. In a film script, the emphasis is on the visual which relays the scene settings and hopefully the exposition in cinematic form. The screenplay developed from the silent period of Hollywood, when separate writers wrote the story-line and others wrote the title cards containing the dialogue. Films place less reliance on talking, therefore the form follows content and gives it less space, which explains why it is squeezed into the middle of the page.

Many of the rules discussed in this excellent book have been developed over the years during the history of cinema. Many rules are still evolving. Some rules are hard and fast, while other rules are creatively allowed to vary. This book designates the differences where possible. Producers are aware of the nuances of form and are finely attuned to the variations in design. Writers who hope to get more impact per page will go beyond the rule to understand what the rule means and learn how to use it properly.

A WELL-PRESENTED SCREENPLAY OFTEN INDICATES SOMETHING ABOUT THE CONTENT

Most producers flip through a script to get a feel for it: Is it thick with scene description? Is it shorter than a hundred pages or longer than 125? Is it designed in theatrical play format (a mistake for a film script) or is it neatly typed? If a writer knows the rule of thumb that a page of script is equal to a minute on the screen, then a script will be properly paced by design. If a writer knows that a page of action/chase should look different than a witty page of cocktail chatter, then the writer will design more scene description for the action and more dialogue for the party. If a writer knows that the design of the page is critical, then no important jokes, no important ideas and no important concepts will be buried in the middle of block scene descriptions. A well designed script flows with the reading and accentuates the pacing.

If a script is well typed, well designed, then the producer has a feeling that the author might have a grasp on the content, style, and dialogue. However, if the screenplay is written with the wrong design, it may be an indication that the author is only a beginner, unable to handle the content as well.

Unfortunately, many students are not aware that most published screenplays are published in the wrong formats. Simon and Schuster uses the transposition into play format for its Modern Film Script Series. Three major screenplays (Ox-Bow Incident, High Noon. and Lilies of the Field) published by Globe Book Company, Inc. uses the dialogue spread across the full page. This is correct for theatrical plays today but not currently used in film scripts. Even the recent prestigious publication of the Screenplay Library Series by the Southern Illinois University Press which does use screenplay format for the dialogue (down the middle of the page) violates the page-a-minute concept by not transposing the length of a page from the original script. The format indicates photographs are included in the script format. Maps, illustrations, and photos may accompany the written material but are never included inside the covers of a script. This is based on the idea that the words must convey the ideas within the script.

Any student of screenwriting who follows the format of most published screenplays will find himself in trouble with prospective producers at first glance. A producer is able to "eyeball" a script by its design and separate out these amateur efforts. Certainly good story and effective dialogue will win the producer over to a sale, but a beginning writer needs everything helping him... especially format.

Many beginning writers get a knowledgeable typing service to transpose their script into the correct cinematic design, but this is a surface treatment. There is a closer connection between form and content which the writer should not ignore. As with poetry, the placement of the word on the page says a lot about the impact of the content. If an important idea is hidden in a jumble of scene description a typing service will correct only the margins and tab settings, they will not extricate the ideas and redesign the page, placing the important concepts in prominent positions. This is the job of the writer alone.

This book is about the rules of the page design. It is not about the content or narrative of the film. Yet, a writer must know about the design of the page if the content is to be presented properly. This book is an extensive discussion about the enhancement of content. This is an important key to the success of a screenplay.

AN IMPORTANT CONCEPT; SCRIPT WRITING IS WRITING-BY-LENGTH

The finite form of a screenplay can be compared to the finite form of a sonnet or a Haiku poem. The screenplay is a page-a-minute which restricts the two hour feature to approximately 120 pages. The one hour teleplay for an episodic show is about 54 pages considering the time left for commercials.

It is an important concept that a screenplay is paced. The length of the screenplay is almost predetermined. What happens on approximately page thirty is equivalent to the thirtieth minute into the film. It is a bit unnerving to novelists attempting a screenplay to hear the corrections. "Put more action on page eight and replace the surprise on page thirty." It is a shock to hear specific page references, but often producers have a sense of pacing for the desired show and want a specific moment of drama on a specific page.

Often beginning writers sit down at the typewriter or computer to pour their very thoughts onto the script page leaving it cluttered and out of kilter with the necessary pacing. This is a mistake. A screenplay does not have room for excessive details. While a novelist or short story writer might establish the character's identity by listing all the items in his or her bathroom cabinet (a technique enjoyed by J.D. Salinger among others), a screenwriter does not have the luxury of expandable length to the written material.

If a beginning writer wanted to describe a person's first day at the office, it would not be correct screenplay writing to list every item on the desks, every paper clip, every calendar on the wall, every potted plant, every blotter, every water cooler, etc., etc., etc. A writer does not make a grocery list of what will be seen on the screen. If the bottom of the page is approximately what happens at the end of the first minute there is no room to detail every prop to be set by the art director.

ANOTHER IMPORTANT CONCEPT (RELATED TO FORM): A PAGE IS A SUMMARY OF THE MINUTE OF SCREEN TIME

The ephemera of the actual page (the ink itself and the paper itself) is different than the experience of the minute.

The piece of film is a series of visual images (24 frames per second) with a sound track and it is meant to be projected and viewed. The page is meant to be read. The experiences are different and the internal times are different. It only takes about fifteen or twenty seconds to read a well-designed page while it takes a whole minute to view the film.

To take things further, a minute of projected time may contain real time inside the fiction of the story or it may be extended or collapsed time within the fiction. A minute of screening time might project a montage of a presidential candidate's rise to the top (a period of months collapsed via the montage to a single minute of screening time). Or a baseball play may be replayed within the minute of projecting time so that the few seconds can be repeated or expanded to fill the minute.

A script page	=	Reading time	=	Projection time	=	Fictional time
eleven inches		Approx 25 sec.		one minute		variable

This is a complicated equation and after it is initially grasped by writers, it is tucked into the back of their minds and seemingly ignored. The essence is the concept that a page of script must be designed for easy reading. That's easy enough to remember.

Reading a script is a bit like viewing a film. The pages should be turned constantly and uniformly the way the film is projected smoothly without ever turning back.

It is not possible to put all the words needed to describe the visuals in an author's head onto the screenplay page and still keep the equation in balance. Even though the fiction time is collapsible, the page-a-minute concept must be maintained.

In the example of the person coming to an office, the plot material must be in the proper layout. One could not take three or four pages to describe the setting before the first character entered the set. In that bad example too many words (pencils, paper clips, wallpaper, desk sizes, etc., etc., etc.) would throw off the pacing.

Here is an example of the difficulty of this concept: Let's say that you are writing a screenplay about some college freshmen who have been away from their Fraternity House on a Friday night looking for the perfect co-ed and they return (on the middle of page 27) to their Frat House to catch a glimpse of this gorgeous young woman. She happens to be coming from within their own Frat House, she pauses in the doorway and then runs away after a brief moment. This is a comedy, of course, but a proper scene for the example.

The important idea is that the young woman is only on view for the briefest of moments. Yet, as the author you may have many, many words to describe this young woman. You have prepared well and have a detailed character sketch. You have some five hundred words to describe this perfect co-ed this female perfection, this vision of loveliness, this delicious confection. Whatever cliches you may have in mind to describe this young woman, you may <u>not</u> use all of them.

How long is the woman on the screen? A brief second! Then the script page would warrant an inch or two at most.

If this were a novel, you would be allowed to use all the words you wanted. This is screenplay writing and it is designed and restricted and placed in a specific pacing format. Time equals length. If she is glimpsed briefly, then she appears on the page briefly.

The solution is to summarize her appearance to fit within the space allowed.

In the previous example of the office worker's first day, if the person arrives at the office at the beginning of the first minute of the film, the character appears at the appropriate place on the script page. Kiss those three pages of pencils, clips, etc., goodbye. There is no room for grocery list descriptions.

These concepts about the uniqueness of script writing are often shocking to the beginning screenwriter. They ask about the reverse situation, where there is time to fill and the words are not in their minds. What about the three minute bar-room fight in a western film script? Do they have to fill three pages?

Yes, approximately. But the beginning writer begins to squirm, what if they don't have the words. I answer that their job is to choreograph the pacing of the scene (not the actual fight itself, which will be the stunt man or director's job). It is their job to fill the time with ideas, showing the progress of the bar-room fight while manipulating the emotions of the author. More often than not, the director will not use the specific suggestions of the author but parallel the ideas with whatever is available on the film set. The result will be an approximation of the overall concept.

The above examples demonstrate the uniqueness of screenwriting. In the Fraternity House and First Day At The Office examples, the writer had more words than space allowed. In the last example of the bar-room fight, there were more pages than words. The author had to adjust to accommodate the nature of the screenplay. Content had to be deleted or added to conform to the format of the pacing.

ANOTHER CONCEPT: IN SCREENPLAY WRITING IT IS NOT NECESSARY TO WRITE ACROSS THE PAGE. ONE MAY WRITE DOWN THE PAGE

All screenplays are typewritten (rather than handwritten or typeset). The words are placed in specific positions on an 8 1/2" by 11" page. (The British screenplays use a legal length page). There are only a few components of the screenplay page: Slug lines or Scene Headings, Scene Descriptions, Character Names, Dialogue, Opticals and in a very few instances Personal Direction (line reading instructions which are frowned upon by actors and directors who want to use their own interpretation of lines). For a further explanation of these components and their functions, read the book!

A screenwriter does not have unlimited space. Length down the page is as important as the concept of page length into the script. It is important to know where something should be placed on the page. Opticals are not placed where dialogue is supposed to go. Proper placement, spacing, double spacing, capitalization and underlining are some of the techniques open to the writer to enhance the content.

One hundred twenty pages is a very short length and it must be layered to get across the correct information. Not only must the content be presented, the placement of the content must deliver information about pacing. Sentences do not need to be placed after one another as in fiction writing if another placement would deliver more information to the script.

If a writer wants to describe a bar-room fight and has several ideas to get across, it may not be necessary to place the ideas side by side. For example, the author would like to say: "Bart stormed into the saloon. He grabbed a bottle and broke it on the bar rail. Then he began a stand-off with the other man, Carl."

That content is very clear. A man comes in and prepares to fight a second man with a broken bottle as a weapon. A familiar scene in western films. The task of the screenwriter is to design the page. On the script page, there is a difference between the following two examples:

TECHNIQUE A

INT. BAR - DAY

Bart storms into the saloon. He grabs a bottle and breaks it on the bar rail. He advances across the floor. It is a stand-off with Carl.

TECHNIQUE B

INT. BAR - DAY

Bart storms into the saloon.

He grabs a bottle and breaks it on the bar rail.

Then he advances across the floor.

It is a stand-off with Carl.

Notice that Technique (B) places the simple sentences underneath each other. It is a technique to use up the minute. It highlights the important action. It is a summary of the events within the fictional time frame and it is easy to scan while reading the script. Obviously the entire page will be a summary of the minute's action.

If you are wondering, yes, it is a valid method of screenwriting popular with some writers in Hollywood not used by others. Walter Hill (<u>Hard Times</u>, <u>Alien</u>, <u>The Long Riders</u>) likes to work in this style, to name a specific writer among many.

Technique (A) is closer to the novelist's technique and it is a slower form to read. The scene would be filled with more details, placing the breaking of the bottle into a minor incident in the overview of the minute's action. One might suspect that the dialogue would be forthcoming from Bart and Carl during the stand-off, which explains the format of Technique A (action is not the important part of the minute) whereas in Technique B, action is all important and there may be no dialogue on the rest of the page. The bottle breaking is an important symbol in the minute, deserving more space on the page.

The content and the words are the same but the format or design of the page places a different emphasis on both examples.

A WARNING: A SCRIPT GOES THROUGH SEVERAL VERSIONS

There are various versions or rewriting patchworks done to a script after it leaves the hands of a writer. This sounds shocking to a playwright who has respect given to his language in the play script. In contrast, the screenwriter usually sells control of his script, giving the producer or studio legal permission to change it. Much has been written about this "translation" to the screen and it is not appropriate to debate it in this foreword, except to note that it does happen.

For the purposes of references within this book, it will be assumed that a model script goes through all the possible sets of revisions. Consider for theoretical purposes:

<u>Version One is the Author's Version</u>. This may encompass several rewrites, but consider them all as the author's work. Then it is sold.

<u>Version Two may be the Director or Producer's Version</u>. When they buy a script, they may add in camera angles or delete expensive passages when it is budgeted. They may not change the dialogue or the scene description but

merely regroup it into practical and filmable scenes.

(It is important to note that many producers, directors, studios, and agents plead with beginning writers not to include camera angles or specific music cues. These should not be part of the script until it has been sold and the director determines which camera style will be used and the producer has an idea of the budget available for music rights. Take warning, beginning writers... stick to the story, the characterizations, the dialogue, and the form, but not the specifics of a non-writing department.)

<u>Version Three may be the Studio Version</u>. The producer will try to get financing and perhaps package the script, that is, place it with a star or include commercial elements which will have marquee value to draw in customers. It may be necessary to change some of the elements of the script to accommodate these new elements (changing it to a new location, changing a bit of dialogue to fit a star's personality).

<u>Version Four is the Set Version</u>. If there is an improvised scene done before the cameras, it is possible that the studio will ask a secretary to type up a copy of the filmed scene to insure the script is a correct historical log of the shooting. These corrected pages may be distributed to the cast and crew days after the scene has been finished.

<u>Version Five may be the Legal Version</u>. Once the film is in proper shape for release, the studio may have a copy typed up from the released film print. Someone will observe the print in a stop-and-go projection room so that every bit of exact dialogue and every exact cut can be preserved on paper. This version is done on legal sized paper and the secretary's version of the action is down the left side of the page. A copy of this version is deposited in the Library of Congress.

<u>Version Six may be the Published Version</u>, which is squashed into play format, as previously discussed. The redesign of the film's script is done with little regard for the page-a-minute pacing. Ignoring the format of the author's version, they reach for the legal version and print a secretary's description of the action in their own format. This results in a distorted impression of a script, which explains the hybrid results done by many beginning writers who rely on these published versions.

REMEMBER...

Producers, directors, agents, and even screenplay instructors plead with students not to include camera angles in their scripts. The director will ignore them and they take up important space within the format of the page. Just because some publishers reprint scripts from the legal copy of the script, it does not mean that those were the words used by the author to get the script sold. The camera angles may have been added after production meetings by the director.

While this book includes information about camera angles, personal direction, songs, etc., it does not mean that beginning scriptwriters should include such elements in their scripts. For example, scene numbers usually mean that a script has been budgeted. Any beginning screenwriter who is seeking an agent probably has not had his or her script budgeted, and it is presumptuous to pretend that it has happened. Therefore, the script for sale must look a certain way. It should be easy to read and focus on the story line, not the specifics of production.

Because this is a thorough book, all typing instructions have been included, but TAKE WARNING, do not include camera angles in a selling screenplay unless you have a deal with a specific director or production company which has given you permission.

Enjoy this book. It contains the keys to unlocking the uniqueness of screenplay writing. It is a tool to be used in placing a professional look to your script page. It is part of the state of the art of screenplay literature. There is no comparable book which goes into such depth about format.

James F. Boyle, Ph.D.
Former Screenwriting Instructor
Cinema Department
University of Southern California

TABLE OF CONTENTS

Page   CONTENTS

(1)   SOME WORDS ABOUT THE IMPORTANCE OF SCRIPTS AND FORMATS
(2)   WORDS FOR NEW WRITERS
(3)   HOW TO USE THIS MANUAL
          HELPS FOR SETTING UP FORMATS ON THE P.C.
(4)   Pitch and point size explained
(4)   Line length explained
(5)   About tabs, margins and indents

(6)   WHAT ARE FILMED SHOWS?
(7)   Definitions of general terms
(9)   Format Comparison Chart

         PRELIMINARIES - GENERAL INFORMATION
(10)   Checking out the Script
(11)   Typewriter settings: margins and tabs

(13)   COVER DESIGN
(14)   Samples for screenplays
(18)   Samples for filmed series

         TITLE/FLY PAGE LAYOUT
(19)   Laying out the title/fly page: What, where, how
(20)   Sample for filmed television series

         HOW TO GET INTO THE FIRST PAGE AND PROCEED
(21)   First page - feature films (no acts)
(21)   First page - filmed television show - in acts
(23)   First page - filmed series with episode title - in acts
              First page - Act Two
              The second page - no acts and Act One, Act Two

         SCENE HEADINGS: HOW TO PUT SCENE HEADINGS IN THE
            PROPER SEQUENCE
(26)   Preliminaries
(26)   Format rules
(29)   How to put each scene entry in correct order and form
(29)   Two entry scene heading/master scene
(31)   How to number scenes without leaving a scene out: Spotting errors
(33)   What information do you enclose in parentheses
(36)   Examples of scene headings you will want to know
(43)   Exercise and answer key

Page	CONTENTS
	SCENE HEADINGS: HOW TO TAKE A SCENE FROM ONE PAGE TO ANOTHER
(47)	With scene numbers - use of CONTINUED
	Without scene numbers
(49)	When the scene runs for three or more pages
(51)	**SCENE ENDINGS/TRANSITIONS: HOW TO END SCENES**
	Preliminaries
	Format
	At the end of an act
	At the end of the show
	At all other times
	FADE IN/FADE OUT, FREEZE FRAME rules
	Notes: FADE TO:
	STAGE DIRECTION: KNOW WHAT TO CAPITALIZE
(53)	Preliminaries
	Format
(55)	Sound cues
	Spotting Errors
(57)	Camera Cues
	Spotting Errors
(59)	Character introductions
	Spotting Errors
(61)	(a) AD LIB
	(b) TITLES of books, songs, and movies
	(c) VOICE OVER
	(d) BEGIN/END TITLES
	(e) FREEZE FRAME
(63)	Note to the director, technicians
	Spotting Errors
	No capitalization for enter and exit
	STAGE DIRECTION: KNOW WHAT TO ABBREVIATE
	General comments
	b.g., f.g., o.s.
	STAGE DIRECTION: MISCELLANEOUS NOTES
(67)	When paragraphing occurs
	Breaks in sentences: the ellipsis and two dashes
	Rule for breaking direction from one page to next
	Use of FLASHBACKS
(69)	Composite and Exercises and Key

Page	CONTENTS
	THE CHARACTER CUE: IDENTIFYING CHARACTERS
(75)	Preliminaries
	Format Rules
	(a) Abbreviating personal titles
	(b) Using (V.O.) and (O.S.)
(77)	(c) Specific roles are in parentheses
(79)	(d) Spotting Errors
	PERSONAL DIRECTION
(81)	Preliminaries
	Format
(83)	How to "pull out" long passages
	Spotting Errors
	(a) Personal direction under the wrong character cue
(85)	(b) Don't end a page with personal direction
	DIALOGUE
(87)	Preliminaries
	Format
(89)	Follow precise spelling and grammatical rules
	(a) spell out
	(b) hyphen
	(c) breaking to next page
	(d) pause
	(e) ellipsis
	(f) dash
	(g) paragraphing
	BREAKING DIALOGUE
(91)	When to use (MORE)
	How to use (CONT'D)
	BREAKING DIALOGUE: (continuing)
(93)	(continuing) after stage direction - middle of the page
	(continuing) after stage direction - bottom of the page
(95)	(continuing) and (beat) are related
	When (continuing) is not necessary
(98)	**SCREENPLAY COMPOSITES**
(103)	Standard shooting script
(107)	Reading script

THE FILM IN PRODUCTION

(111)	**GENERAL INTRODUCTORY MATERIAL**

TABLE OF CONTENTS (CONT'D)

Page   CONTENTS

(112)   HOW TO HANDLE REVISION PAGES
                    Revisions: Pages are color coded
                    Revisions: Always "hold" page and scene numbers
(113)   (a) All page and scene numbers must be accounted for
                    (b) What are "A" pages
                    (c) What are "runs"
                    How to add or omit scenes
                    Spotting Errors
(115)   Revision headings (slugs) vary with production companies
(117)   Asterisks: How to use asterisks to indicate changes
                       on revision pages
                    Asterisks: Preliminary information
                    Asterisks: Line change only
                    Asterisks: The two-thirds rule
                    (a) Asterisk by character cue when...
                    (b) Asterisk by scene number when...
                    (c) Asterisk by page number when...
(119)   Asterisks: Omitted lines or paragraphs
                    Asterisks: Exceptions
(122)   Revision/Asterisk Exercise with Key

          HOW TO CONSTRUCT A SHOOTING SCHEDULE FROM BREAKDOWN SHEETS
(134)   Preliminaries
(135)   General Information
                    Format - First page
(137)   Format - Body
(138)   Miscellaneous items
(139)   Sample Schedule - Heading information
(141)   Breakdown sheets - Explanation
(142)   Sample breakdown sheets
(151)   Sample shooting schedule typed in correct format

(154)   GLOSSARY

(161)   APPENDIX

SOME WORDS ABOUT THE IMPORTANCE
OF SCRIPTS AND SCRIPT FORMATS

The script is the basic tool of the movie and television industry. No script, no show. No matter how spontaneous a television show or film may seem, you can be absolutely sure that there was a script involved. Scripts are used for everything from game shows to talk shows to charity telethons to documentaries.

And so, important as it is that there be a script, equally important is the necessity for that script to be written in the correct standard format appropriate for a given filming situation. A one camera film production requires a specific script format quite different from a three camera television production.

The standard script formats which are universally used in the movie and television industry today have evolved because each one is designed to suit a specific filming situation. Therefore, script formats are not just randomly spaced words scattered on a page. Each script format is logically and concisely planned to accommodate the unique aspects of a particular filming situation. One can well imagine that it would be utterly impossible to gather up a novel and a camera, go out on location, and shoot a film. The book must be re-written -- translated if you will -- into a film format script. No easy job, as is attested to by the fact that those who are talented at this formidable task receive Academy Awards for screen adaptations!

Since formats vary to accommodate a specific filming circumstance, it is by the same token true that one cannot make a film format into a three camera television format by merely changing the spacing and re-setting the typewriter tabs. Film formats and television formats are not interchangeable. Translating from one format to another requires a (frequently major) rewrite of the entire script. (See Format Comparison Chart Pg. 9)

There are many reasons for adhering strictly to a consistent standard format. A given script must serve as a basic tool which is used by many hands -- directors, technicians, actors, and many others. It must serve as a handle which each can easily catch hold of to facilitate that filming endeavor. The right tool must be used for the right job.

Not only does a standard format provide a framework and essential guideline for a specific filming technique, it also serves as an indicator for timings. One script page in proper format generates approximately one minute of "screen time".

Standard Script Formats, however, involve much more than typewriter tab settings and correct spacings. Hence, the necessity for a manual such as this. What follows in these pages are the nuts and bolts of Standard Script Formats.

In the beginning this volume was designed to serve a broad range of individuals involved with scripts: script personnel in production situations, those hoping to type scripts professionally, seasoned writers and new writers, and everyone in between. But in recent years film and cinema programs have carved a significant place in college and university curriculums, and screenwriting seminars flourish. Therefore, it's important to address specific information necessary for beginning writers.

If you are a new screenwriter, your chances of selling your script are predicated on having an agent. In our many interviews with literary agents, professional script readers, and teachers of screenwriting, the consensus is that they require reading script form from new writers. This means a script with standard line lengths and spacing but devoid of most technical instructions. (Most scripts you have read have undoubtedly been shooting scripts which are detailed in this book.)

Use master scenes (INT. and EXT.), few if any shots and angles, and minimal direction. Agents want to see white when they read a script. This means dialogue. If you write too much direction they see red. They want to concentrate on your writing skills and are distracted when you add too many technicalities. This form is advantageous to you because the absence of technicalities allows more space for the creative/writing aspect of your screenplay.

Here are the DO'S and DON'T'S for reading scripts. Page numbers under the DO'S reference what should be done. Page numbers referenced in the DON'T'S refer you to what should be avoided.

THE DO'S FOR A READING SCRIPT

Use standard line lengths for direction and dialogue (p. 4,5,11,53)
Use standard spacing between scenes, direction, dialogue
Focus on dialogue, the vehicle that carries the story
Stay within acceptable page count (approximately 100 - 115)

THE DON'T'S

No scene numbers
No shots/angles unless ABSOLUTELY necessary for clarification
  (p. 26)
No scene endings/transitions (CUT TO:, DISSOLVE TO:) (p.51)
No scene CONTINUEDS tops/bottoms of page (p. 47)
No capping in direction (p. 53-58, 61-64)
Avoid standard abbreviated terms in direction (p. 65)
Avoid personal (parenthetical) direction to the character except
  where clarification is ABSOLUTELY necessary (p. 82-86)
No (continuing) under character name. (p. 93).

Pages 102 - 110 show the basic difference between a shooting script and a reading script.

HOW TO USE THIS MANUAL

This book does not belong strictly to the liberal arts. It does not teach creative writing. It is more suited to the manual arts, for it is a book about form and the rules that apply to that form. The form is called a script. This book will show you how to form your creative ideas into a standard script form. It will teach you how to build a script. Like poetry formats, script formats must be mastered completely so as not to restrict the art but to make if fulfill its intended purpose.

So this is a manual, a how-to-do-it book. It is designed to be used as a text for the classroom. A person familiar with format can use it as an easy reference for format details. For others, it can be a self-teaching tool. Exercises and their keys, quick reference sheets to keep at your typewriter, a glossary, and an index -- all make this book suitable to almost every need.

The completed two volume manual will cover four formats: Film, Three-Camera Tape, Tape Live, and Variety shows. Revisions, shooting and taping schedules, short and long rundowns are included as a part of these basic formats.

At this point please take time to read through the table of contents, keeping the following in mind. It you were to pick up a script and start reading, the cover would be first, then the title/fly page, then the first page of the script. Note that the table of contents is ordered in the same way. Continuing then with the script, you would read the first page heading, the opening scene heading, some stage direction, a character's cue, dialogue and so on. The contents follow that same order.

Now read through the contents.

The contents give you a good idea of the material. Now notice the layout of the text itself by flipping through the pages. With few exceptions, all exposition is on the left; all examples illustrating the text are on the right. We have tried to "keep it simple". Examples are placed at the correct tab settings using a word processing 10 pitch, 12 point (height) font which produces the same type size and style as the Courier 72, 10 pitch IBM typewriter element in order that you may become accustomed to seeing the various parts of the screenplay properly placed on the page. This visualizing should assist you greatly in learning.

WORD PROCESSING/P.C. CONSIDERATIONS

Word processors and personal computers are here to stay. They greatly simplify rewriting and editing. But they don't do all.

While script formatting programs expedite page endings, breaking direction and dialogue appropriately (always at the end of a sentence) and numbering scenes if required, there are limitations. With a few macros, formatting programs are not really necessary to set up correct spacing or margins and tabs to create the proper line lengths, a significant factor in standard industry format.

PITCH AND POINT SIZE

Type/font size is most important. Pitch means the number of letters and characters per inch. Ten pitch = 10 letters per inch. Ten pitch type is what standard script formats are based on. The examples used in this book on the right hand pages are Courier 10 pitch type.

Point size refers only to the height of the letters and has traditionally been a typesetting consideration. If your computer requires a point size choice as well as designating 10 pitch, 12 point is the correct point size for height.

SETTING MARGINS AND TABS TO CREATE PROPER LINE LENGTH

The following information is offered in attempt to get the correct format set up on your computer. By no means is this intended as a magic formula for creating a word processing screenplay format program. No quick easy way. Using WordPerfect software the following guidelines will at least get you started:

Perhaps the most useful key to setting up correct format is to determine line lengths. This simply involves counting the number of characters and spaces.

DIRECTION: 55 characters and spaces

DIALOGUE: 35 characters and spaces
(The above line is 35 characters/spaces.)

PERSONAL DIRECTION: 16 characters and spaces

Besides setting tabs it is crucial to set the right margin to achieve the correct line length. Otherwise direction and dialogue lines will not cut off and wrap to the next line at the right place.

TAB AND INDENT

The tab key is used for the character name, personal (parenthetical) direction under the character name, and scene endings or transitions such as CUT TO; or (CONTINUED).

Since personal direction may be more than one line, hard returns
should be used to control the correct line lengths. The tab key
is used for any entity that should not automatically wrap around.

The shift/indent function is used for direction and dialogue to
allow for the automatic cut off and wrap around to the next line.

Shift/indent keys indent equally from left and right margins and
wrap lines to the correct tab setting. Never use hard returns to
dictate direction and dialogue line lengths throughout a script.
First, it defeats the technology of the computer as a fast and
efficient help and second, it makes editing and rewrites a
nightmare.

MACROS

Storing in macros recurring information such as major character
names and key functions such as left/right indents saves time.
Storage in a macro using the alt shift plus a letter on the key
pad is easier and faster.

Also create macros that include spacing and indents for the most
used elements of scripts: Scene/shot heading, direction, transitions, character, personal direction and dialogue. Separate
macros for each main character is also a big timesaver.

SUGGESTIONS FOR GETTING STARTED (All can be stored in one macro
to be used each time you start a new document.)

1. TURN OFF JUSTIFICATION. (Looks nice but not in scripts.)

2. TURN OFF HYPHENATION. (Hyphenation is not used in dialogue.
    Hyphenation in direction is easily done manually.)

3. CREATE A HEADER to carry the automatic page numbering at the
    top right side of each page.

4. TOP AND BOTTOM MARGINS 1/2 inch (.50")

5. LEFT MARGIN 1 inch / RIGHT MARGIN 3/4 inch (.75")

6. TAB SETTINGS

1"	1.6"	2.6"	3.3"	3.9"	5.9"	7.2"
Left Margin	Direc-tion	Dialogue	Personal Direction	Character Name	Trans-itions	Pg. #

Note: These elements (dialogue, character names, etc.) may not
fall exactly on the page compared with placement on a page of
standard format. But as long as it's not drastically off and as
long as the spacing and line lengths are correct, the page count
will be accurate. P.C. programs require creative jockeying.

A filmed show may be a feature length movie to be shown at a movie theater, a movie made for television or an action television series filmed on location. Such series shows include "Perry Mason", "Matlock", "In the Heat of the Night", and "Northern Exposure".

The terms Filmed Show, Screenplay, One-camera, and Feature Films are used interchangeably to mean a production filmed on location. This means that the exterior scenes are shot outside on various locations: the beach, a carnival, a tenement, a car chase on a Los Angeles street. Frequently, part of the production crew will go to a designated locale and shoot some of the exteriors before the actors and production personnel arrive. Consequently, filmed shows are not shot in the same sequential order as the script.

Filmed shows rarely consist of exteriors alone. Understandably, there are scenes which take place indoors. Many interiors such as inside an architecturally interesting building or a restaurant will be shot on location. Recurring buildings and areas in a television series are shot on a studio set.

It is this location aspect of filmed shows which basically dictates the standard script format used for all film productions and differentiates film format from television (tape) format. (See Format Comparison Chart, page 9)

Following are some definitions of basic terms you will want to know. These along with others can be found in the glossary.

DEFINITIONS OF A FEW GENERAL TERMS
NEEDED BEFORE PROCEEDING

STAGE DIRECTION — Any information describing a setting or location, situation, character, technical instruction, lengthy personal direction, and the like.

CHARACTER CUE — A name or sometimes a title or description used to assign lines of dialogue.

PERSONAL DIRECTION — Those specific and usually short personal instructions intended for a particular character which appear in parenthesis just under the character cue. Examples: (nods), (sits down), (trembling with fear).

DIALOGUE — Words spoken by any given character. Includes also those times when he is "thinking out loud", talking over the phone, or talking from another room.

SOUND CUE — A sound requiring the technical reproduction services of a sound technician. Sound cues usually appear in stage direction and must be spotlighted by capitalization.

CAMERA CUE — A specific instruction given to the camera. Camera cues appear in stage direction and must be spotlighted by capitalization.

VOICE OVER (V.O.) — The mechanical transmission of an off screen voice such as a voice over the telephone or a voice over a P.A. system or a voice over a tape recorder. Stated: VOICE OVER in stage direction and (V.O.) next to a character cue.

(O.S.) off screen — A voice (or sound) heard coming from another room, while the camera is on another subject. The person speaking off screen is readily available to be on camera.

Always abbreviated.

ON TO THE SCRIPT!

Basic differences between Filmed
formats and Taped television formats.

FILMED FORMAT (Features and action/ location TV Shows)	TAPED FORMAT (Sitcoms, Variety shows, Game shows, Talk shows, etc.)
Mainly filmed on locations with the interior scenes shot either on location or in a studio.	Shot exclusively in a studio. Nearly all scenes are interiors.
Movie Camera more portable & versatile for location filming.	TV Camera more cumbersome & less mobile, but works well on the smooth floor of a studio.
Format: Single spaced with double spacing used to separate elements.	Format: Basically double spaced. Single spacing used only in direction.
Format: Upper/lower case with only scene headings in all CAPS.	Format: All caps with only dialogue in upper/lower case.
Scene Headings: Longer & more detailed, sometimes using camera angles and camera subject, as well as the INT. or EXT. location & time of day.	Scene Headings: Called Set Headings, use only basic information re: INT. and time of day. (EXT. not often used.)
Format: Camera & sound cues CAPPED in direction.	Format: Camera cues underlined in direction. Sound cues capped, isolated at margin, underlined.
Stage Direction accompanying master scenes is longer, more explanatory and detailed.	Stage Direction brief... usually only a few lines.
Dialogue & Direction share job of carrying the story & action.	Dialogue mainly carries the story and action.
Characters: Many involved.	Characters: Only a few. In series, regulars appear consistently.

Before the first page is typed, the following things must be considered:

FIRST   Is it necessary to number the scenes? If the work is a
          first draft and is intended for presentation, it is probably
          not necessary nor in fact advisable to number the scenes.
          Some professionals in "the business" feel that scene numbers
          tend to "clutter" up the flow in works that are at the
          presentation stage. It is in fact true that scene numbers
          are rarely necessary in the author's version. Scene numbers
          are assigned after the film has been budgeted.

SECOND   If scene numbers are required, it must be determined whether
          or not they are needed on both sides. Usually not. The
          only time scene numbers are necessary on both sides (left
          and right) is on the final drafts of a shooting script
          currently in production.

THIRD   When typing a screenplay for someone else, (for either love
          or preferably money!) make sure all the pages of the
          original copy are numbered consecutively. This will save
          much anxiety and Alka-Seltzer in the ever present likelihood
          that it is accidentally dropped on the floor.

LAST   When typing any script for someone else, make certain that
          they understand that there is a Standard Script Format for
          that given filming situation which is accepted as gospel in
          the industry. Any deviations therefrom must be spelled out
          very clearly from the beginning. If, for example, someone
          requests that scene headings be underlined, that must be a
          specific request since Standard Format does not dictate that
          this be done.

TYPEWRITER SETTINGS, FILM FORMAT
_____

When typing a script on the typewriter, use the following simpli-
fied margins and tab settings. The left edge of the paper should
be at number one on the typewriter index.

The following tabs should be set:

        19   Direction (cut off at 73)
        29   Dialogue (cut off at 60)
        36   Personal direction (cut off at 55)
        43   Character cue
        62   Scene ending/scene (CONTINUED)
        72   Page number

If scene numbers are used on the left, set the margin at 13. If
scene numbers are also used on the right, set a tab at 74. Note
that the right side scene numbers are off set a couple of spaces
so that they are not confused with the page number.

Remember that scenes shouldn't be numbered in reading scripts or
first draft scripts. Scene numbering is really the director's
job anyway.

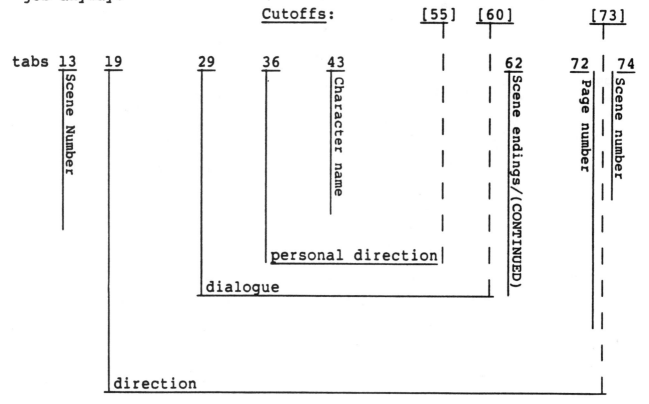

HELPFUL HINT: The first letter of the character name over dialogue
should fall exactly in the left to right center of the page. Fold the
page in half longways to check.

COVER DESIGNS

SCREENPLAYS AND FILMED SERIES

SCREENPLAY COVER DESIGN

A screenplay ready to present as a feature length film or a television movie of the week (MOW) should be bound in heavy covers both front and back using brass fasteners to secure it. The cover weight should be at least 65 pound index. This simply means that the cover should be of a heavier stock than the paper in the script which is 20 pound weight.

The title of the work is usually the only information that is needed on the cover of a screenplay or a television movie. Occasionally a production company will request the name of the company as well. Additional information such as the author, draft, date or an address should be placed on the fly (title) page directly following the cover.

There are a number of optional methods that may be used to indicate the title on a cover. It may be inexpensively "printed" by a script or copy service using a quick setup type available in different sizes and styles. Or you can use press-on letters available at art and stationery stores. Another viable alternative is to create the title art work yourself using a black marking pen on a white sheet of paper stylizing the title appropriate to the content of the script. All these methods of camera ready art can be run onto cover stock with high quality copy machines. The results can be most satisfactory.

Whatever method is used, the title should appear, in appropriate-sized letters dictated to title length, one third of the way down from the top of the page. (approximately 20 to 25 lines) It should be centered left to right.

NOTE: Illustrations, pictures, maps, and other "fluff" do not belong in the script or on the cover. If you decide that any of these visuals are absolutely necessary, include them in a separate package. Don't clutter up the cover of the script with it.

PRINTED TITLE

HONG KONG HARRY

COVERS: FILMED SERIES

FILMED SERIES COVER DESIGN

Covers used on scripts for television series productions usually utilize heavy stock. Occasionally, lighter weight covers may be used instead. Either way, the cover will contain much more information -- information that ordinarily would be found on a fly page. There is a practical reason for doing this. In series film television shows, several scripts may be dealt with simultaneously, so it's more convenient to place all the pertinent information on the cover. There, it is more quickly and easily seen, and helps prevent someone from grabbing the wrong script.

FINAL DRAFT
May 5, 1980

NBC

LITTLE HOUSE ON THE PRAIRIE

"Portrait of Love"

by

Michael Landon

Story No. L.H. 171

Prod. No. 7655

NBC Productions, Inc.

LAYING OUT THE FLY (TITLE) PAGE

What, where, how?

The fly (or title page, either term is correct) immediately follows the cover of the script and contains some or all of the following basic information:

1) Title - Line 25, centered, in caps.
Quotes and underscoring may be used if desired.

2) Written by - Line 30, centered

3) Author - Line 32, centered

4) Draft - Line 55, approximately at Tab 62. (Optional information since a draft designation is not "required")

5) Date - Line 60, same tab as draft. (Optional information)

At Margin 15:

6) Production Company or management company or individual name

7) Address

8) Phone number (optional)

The last line of information should end no lower than line 60.

(See Example 20A opposite)

NOTE: It is not necessary to place the Writers Guild registration on the script. However, many prefer to place it there and to do so is quite acceptable.

20A

"A LAPSE OF MEMORY"

Written by

Natasha Petroff

COLE-MINE PRODUCTIONS
711 Bluebird Lane
Hollywood, California 91000
(213) 874-4900

REVISED FINAL DRAFT
December 25, 1980

HOW TO GET INTO THE FIRST PAGE
OF THE SCRIPT AND PROCEED

The first page of a film script may or may not be numbered. All pages thereafter are numbered. The first page always distinguishes itself from all others because of the heading information which should appear. Format differences between a feature film and a television film series occur because of the type and amount of information required. The format for these various considerations follow.

NOTE: There must be a FADE IN: at the beginning of each act and a FADE OUT. at the end of that act. The same is true when there are no acts. The first page must FADE IN: and the last page, the end, must FADE OUT. FADE IN: and FADE OUT. must be used concurrently.

FIRST PAGE - FEATURE FILM - NO ACTS

    1)   "TITLE" - line 6, centered, in caps and quotes

    2)   FADE IN: - line 10, at tab 19, in caps, colon

    3)   First scene number - line 12, margin 13

(See Example 22A opposite)

FIRST PAGE - FILM TELEVISION SHOW IN ACTS

    1)   "TITLE" - line 6, centered, in caps and quotes

    2)   ACT ONE - line 9, centered, in caps, underlined

    3)   FADE IN: - line 13, at margin 13

    4)   First scene number - line 15, margin 13

(See Example 22B opposite)

22 A - NO ACTS

"THE ESCAPE ARTIST"

FADE IN:

1   EXT. PRISON - DAY

22B - IN ACTS

"JUSTICE ON TRIAL"

ACT ONE

FADE IN:

1   INT. COURTROOM - DAY

<u>HOW TO GET INTO THE FIRST PAGE</u>
<u>OF A FILMED SERIES</u>

<u>FIRST PAGE - FILMED SERIES WITH EPISODE TITLE - IN ACTS</u>

      1)   SERIES TITLE - line 6, centered in caps (no quotes)

      2)   "Episode Title" - line 8, centered, upper/lower case, in quotes

      3)   <u>ACT ONE</u> - line 11, centered, in caps, underlined

      4)   FADE IN: - line 15, at direction tab (19) capitalized, followed by a colon

      5)   First scene number - line 17, at margin (13) (Only the scene number appears at this margin)

           (See Example 24A opposite)

<u>FIRST PAGE - ACT TWO AND ALL SUBSEQUENT ACTS</u>

      1)   Page number - line 4, tab (73) (Only the page number appears at this tab)

      2)   <u>ACT TWO</u> - line 6, centered, in caps, underlined

      3)   FADE IN: - line 10 at (direction) tab (19)

           (See Example 24B opposite)

<u>THE SECOND PAGE - NO ACTS, ACT ONE, ACT TWO</u>

Whether a filmed show is in acts or not, all subsequent pages remain in the same format with the page number on line 4 and either the scene CONTINUED or a new scene heading on line 6.

24A - IN ACTS WITH EPISODE TITLE

BIOGRAPHY OF A PHANTOM

"Incident at Highcliff"

ACT ONE

FADE IN:

1   INT. HIGHCLIFF CASTLE/LIBRARY - NIGHT

24B - ACT TWO & ALL SUBSEQUENT ACTS

ACT TWO

FADE IN:

23   EXT. BRITISH MUSEUM - DAY

ALL ABOUT SCENES

Preliminaries

Scene headings fall into two basic categories: Master Scenes which
are usually general and designated by INT. or EXT. (interior or
exterior) and shots (within the Master Scene) indicating more
specific information such as ANGLES, POV'S, INSERTS, and the like.

Early draft reading scripts should contain few if any shots and
angles to facilitate smoothness and ease of reading. Camera cues
in direction (such as WIDEN TO REVEAL, FIND, MOVE, FOLLOW) may be
used to eliminate the need for many shots but here too, only when
absolutely necessary. Simply write what's happening. Don't
clutter. Make it easy to read so that someone will read it!

Essentially, scene and shot headings are "slugs" of information
used to designate the different segments into which a film
production is broken down. These headings contain basic units of
information needed to film a given scene continuously from
beginning to end in one sequence of shooting.

Scene headings are not only ways to divide up a script for ease of
filming, they essentially convey what the audience should see and
how they should see it.

The majority of all scenes are written from the audience (our)
point of view. The camera is our eyes. It is our window on the
world taking us through a sequence of events and directing our
attention to those things it is important for us to see.

Occasionally, on the other hand, it is effective for us to see
something from a certain character's point of view... to see
someone or something as he sees it. This then becomes a scene
heading stated as a POV shot or Point Of View. (See page 37.)

Each heading is spotlighted by isolating it at the margin in
capital letters with each entity separated by a dash with spaces on
either side. In this way, the basic information contained in each
scene is easily seen at a glance.

Format Rules

   A) All entries in a scene heading are capitalized.

   B) Triple spacing is used between scenes and shots.

   C) A scene heading may NEVER stand alone at the bottom
       of the page. It must be accompanied by at least one
       sentence of direction or a line of dialogue. The
       only EXCEPTION is an ESTABLISHING shot or an INSERT
       discussed in detail later.

Format Rules (Cont'd)

D) The scene heading begins at margin 19. (See Example 28A opposite)

E) Scene headings must cut off at tab 72 so that there is always spaced reserved for the right hand scene number. Whether or not the number on the right side is being used, it will eventually appear there so accommodation must be made for it. (See Example 28B opposite)

F) When a scene heading is particularly long, it must extend to a second line single spaced beneath the heading. If possible it is best to break the heading at a dash. (See Example 28C opposite)

G) Certain words are always abbreviated. These are:

1) INT. and EXT.
2) MED. SHOT or MED. CLOSEUP
3) POV (Point Of View)

Other words such as personal titles may be abbreviated as well. Here, economy of space is especially important.

H) Periods are NEVER used after scene numbers.

I) Normally, scene headings are not underlined.

J) Notice that when the scene takes place in a specific room or area of a building -- house, castle, department store, etc. -- a slash (instead of a dash) may be used to separate these two elements in the scene heading. (See Example 28B and 28C opposite)

```
┌──────────────────────────────────────────────┐
│ 28A - Placement With & Without Scene Numbers   │
└──────────────────────────────────────────────┘
```

    INT. LIBRARY - DAY

7   EXT. LONDON INTERSECTION - NIGHT

```
┌────────────────────────────────────────────┐
│ 28B - Cutoff - Allows For Scene Number On Right │
└────────────────────────────────────────────┘
```

92   EXT. BRANDENBERG CASTLE/COURTYARD - DAY - ON JOEL   92

```
┌──────────────────────────────────────────┐
│ 28C - Scene Heading Extending Two Lines    │
└──────────────────────────────────────────┘
```

57   INT. JOHANNESSON HOUSE/FAMILY ROOM - NIGHT -   57
      CLOSE ON ARTHUR

SCENE HEADINGS: HOW TO PUT EACH
SCENE ENTRY IN CORRECT ORDER
AND FORM

The various elements of a scene heading must be arranged in a specific order:

1) INT. or EXT. LOCATION   2)   TIME OF DAY   3)   CAMERA ANGLE
    4)   WHAT (What the camera is on specifically)

    (See Example 30A opposite)

In other words, WHERE, WHEN, HOW and WHAT. It's easy to remember the correct order if you note that the information progresses from general to specific, or from "large" to "small". The INT. or EXT. LOCATION and the TIME OF DAY are general broad categories narrowing down to the CAMERA ANGLE to the specific CAMERA SUBJECT. The inverted pyramid below will help to visualize this concept.

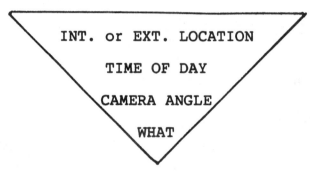

It may be tempting to place the TIME OF DAY as the last entry in a scene slug but this tends to interrupt the flow when a scene heading "feeds" immediately into the direction. When the subject of the camera is the last entry of the heading, the camera subject may also serve as the subject of the first line of direction.

(See Example 30B opposite)

Two Entry Scene Heading

You have probably already concluded that when a scene heading consists only of the LOCATION and TIME OF DAY, the TIME OF DAY will obviously appear as the last entry. (See Example 30C opposite)

This type of heading (the Master Scene) will be used almost exclusively by writers. Intermediate scene headings incorporating camera angles will be "plugged in" later by the director or producer.

30A - Scene Heading - Correct Order

EXT. SAN FRANCISCO - DAY - LONG SHOT - GOLDEN GATE BRIDGE

30B - Flow From Scene Heading To Stage Direction

INT. BAKERY - DAY - CLOSE ANGLE - RALPH

as he gazes longingly at the chocolate eclairs.

30C - Two-Entry Scene Heading

EXT. GARDEN OF EDEN - NIGHT

SCENE HEADINGS: HOW TO NUMBER SCENES
WITHOUT LEAVING A SCENE OUT

Understand that scene numbers should not appear on early
drafts of scripts and definitely not on reading scripts.
When scenes do need to be numbered later on, the director
usually does it. However, the task sometimes falls to
production personnel or to professional script typists.
Each scene and shot is numbered consecutively on the left
side of the script. (When a script goes into production,
scene numbers appear on the right side as well.) Shots and
angles may be buried in direction so it requires an eagle
eye to spot those which must be pulled out and isolated.

Spotting Errors

There are necessary shots that are easily missed. Watch
out for: INSERTS and POV shots. After each of these
headings it is necessary to go either BACK TO SCENE (used
as a heading) or on to another scene. (See Examples
opposite)

32A - Incorrect

15   INT. RABBIT HOLE - ON ALICE AND RABBIT

                        ALICE
              "Late" doesn't tell me what
              time it is. Could I see your
              pocket watch?

                        RABBIT
              Certainly -- but hurry, I'm
              late and the Duchess is
              waiting!

16   INSERT - OVERSIZED POCKET WATCH

        which reads 11:45.

                        ALICE
              That's what time it said before.

32B - Correct

15   INT. RABBIT HOLE - ON ALICE AND RABBIT

                        ALICE
              "Late" doesn't tell me what
              time it is. Could I see your
              pocket watch?

                        RABBIT
              Certainly -- but hurry, I'm
              late and the Duchess is
              waiting!

16   INSERT - OVERSIZED POCKET WATCH

        which reads 11:45.

17   BACK TO SCENE

                        ALICE
              That's what time it said before.

SCENE HEADINGS

What Information Do You Enclose In Parentheses?

Sometimes additional clarifying information is appropriate in a scene heading. This information might indicate the year (1812), the time of year (winter), or the time of day (5:45 A.M.) For the most part, this parenthetical information falls directly after the designation of a specific location like a named city. Placed here, it helps the reader imagine NEW YORK CITY (1910) or NEW ENGLAND (LATE FALL)

Other parenthetical information will fall at the end of the scene heading. Technical in nature, this will indicate a specific type of shot that will probably be handled in post production after filming is completed. Stock shots (stills and film footage) are handled in post production since this material is pulled from the film archives. Stock shots are indicated in parentheses at the end of the scene heading.

The consideration in dealing with parenthetical information is to avoid placing two sets of parentheses side by side. Common sense and a sense of what feels right is of great value here. (See Example 3A opposite)

(Stock and establishing shots will be explained in detail later)

34A - Information Enclosed In Parentheses

EXT. THREE PIGS' HOUSE - DAY - (STOCK)

EXT. LONDON (1892) - 221B BAKER STREET - NIGHT

EXT. CAIRO (EARLY '20'S) - DAY - ESTABLISHING - (STOCK)

EXT. PEARL HARBOR (6:15AM) - DAY - ESTABLISHING

THE FOLLOWING ARE EXAMPLES

OF MOST OF THE

SCENE HEADINGS YOU WILL WANT TO KNOW

(a)   INT. BAR - NIGHT

This scene heading establishes the interior of an area
and the time of day. The interior or exterior should
always appear first in the heading followed, in this
case, by the time of day.

(b)   EXT. MANSION - DAY - CLOSE ANGLE - CHARLOTTE

In correct sequence, this shot establishes <u>where</u>,
<u>when</u>, <u>how</u> (camera angle), and <u>what</u> (the specific
camera subject).

Spotting Errors

If the camera angle and camera subject are mistakenly
placed in the opening stage direction, that
information must be brought up and placed correctly as
entries in the heading.

<u>Example: Incorrect</u>

EXT. MANSION - DAY

Close angle on Charlotte as she is about to...

<u>Example: Correct</u>

EXT. MANSION - DAY - CLOSE ANGLE - CHARLOTTE

as she is about to...

(Note that the last dash eliminates the need for the
word "ON" which is in a sense understood.)

(c)   EXT. PARKINS' HOUSE - DAY (1940)

Any pertinent piece of information, usually having to
do with time -- year, season, or hour of day --
appears in parentheses. This parenthetical
information <u>should</u> be placed next to the specific
element of the heading to which it applies. For the
most part it falls at the end of the heading. When
there is more than one entry of parenthetical, the
placement is usually obvious. The rule dictates the
avoidance of two sets of parenthetical information
following one another.

(d)   EXT. LONDON STREET (1916) - DAY - (STOCK)

Notice that the year entry (1916) is part of the location entry and works as a unit. The year refers to a specific time period in London. This unit of information is then separated from the word DAY with a dash since DAY constitutes another element of information. The word (STOCK) refers to the entire heading and is discussed below.

(e)   EXT. LOS ANGELES STREET - DAY - (STOCK)

This heading indicates that this particular scene is available in the film archives and therefore will not require shooting. It, too, is a parenthetical entry but indicates slightly different information than year, season, hour or day.

(Most authors are not in a position to know whether or not a given shot is in the archives. Stock, then, is not often a choice of most authors.)

(f)   INT./EXT. PARKINS' HOUSE - DAY

The use of INT./EXT. means that two adjacent areas will be covered in the scene. Only a subtle camera movement will be required to proceed from one area to another. This may involve a situation wherein a character is inside the house for a few moments and then moves outside the door.

(g)   HARRY'S POV - SKY

This POV shot tells us that we, the audience, are seeing the sky through Harry's eyes or Point Of View which is the camera angle. There must always be a clear indication of whose POV it is (the subject) and what the POV sees (the object). Remember also that eyeballs have a POV.

(h)   BACK TO SCENE

This tells us that there was a short intervening scene which momentarily took us away from the original scene, and that we are now back to that original scene. Sometimes the intervening scene is longer than a few moments but for the most part it is not. BACK TO SCENE is most frequently used after POV shots and INSERT shots. (See "q")

(i)   **TWO SHOT - HOLMES AND WATSON**

Here, both characters are the exclusive subjects with
little or no background detail. Often this heading will
simply read: HOLMES AND WATSON

(j)   **CLOSE SHOT - JULIETTE**

In this scene we see Juliette from the shoulders up.
Little or no background detail is included.

(k)   **MAUDE**

Sometimes a scene heading designates only a character or
subject. It is a perfectly acceptable practice as long as
the character or subject has already been established in
the master scene.

(l)   **ANGLE ON MR. HYDE**

While this is merely a camera angle change within a
particular established area, it nonetheless works as a
scene heading.

(m)   **EXTREME CLOSEUP - ELIZABETH'S LOCKET**

As the term implies, this is a very close shot used to
emphasize some detail.   It is sometimes written,
INCORRECTLY, ECU or XCU. Correctly it must always be
spelled out in caps.

(n)   **MED. SHOT - SCARLETT AND RHETT**

This shot shows these two characters from the waist up and
may include some background detail. (Similar to TWO SHOT)
MED. of course stands for medium and is the only camera
angle which is abbreviated.

(o)   **EXT. LITTLE HOUSE ON THE PRAIRIE - NIGHT - ESTABLISHING**

Established here is a definite location and/or time of
day. It may also, at the same time, be a (STOCK) shot in
that it may already be on file in the film archives.
Important to remember is the fact that an ESTABLISHING
shot may stand completely alone unaccompanied by any stage
direction or dialogue. It merely serves to quickly give
us a point of reference with regard to where we are at a
given time in the story.

EXAMPLES: SCENE HEADINGS

(p)   ANGLE ON DRIVER OF CONVERTIBLE - TRAVELING

This means that this scene is being filmed as the convertible travels along a street. A second car with the camera mounted on top (the camera car) follows behind or travels alongside and films the action.

NOTE: A traveling shot is not to be confused with the camera cue, DOLLY, which appears in direction. When a character or characters are walking down the sidewalk and the camera is to move with them either in front of them or beside them, the scene should be stated to establish the character or characters with the camera cue DOLLY appearing in the direction. DOLLY may, on rare occasions, appear as a heading reading DOLLY SHOT but more often than not it appears in direction.

Example:

ANGLE - DIANE AND KEVIN

DOLLY WITH THEM as they stroll down the boulevard talking excitedly.

(q)   INSERT - CLOSE ON WALL

An INSERT shot will usually depict a specific inanimate object such as a newspaper headline, a map, a photograph, or some other article. Usually it is accompanied by short, explanatory direction but on rare occasions may stand alone. Whenever this heading appears, it is necessary to follow with the next shot going back to the original or previous scene, or to go on to a new scene.

Example:

INSERT - CLOCK ON WALL

which reads 11:00.

BACK TO SCENE

(r)   INTERCUT - JOHN'S LIVING ROOM/MARTHA'S PARLOUR

An INTERCUT is used to indicate two separate scenes simultaneously.   The INTERCUT is often used with phone conversations or to bring two specific locations together to form a scene.   This heading will always require a scene number unless both scenes have been established previously.   If both locations have been established previously, then the INTERCUT is stated as direction.

Example: Intercut used in direction.

INT. JOHN'S LIVING ROOM

John is on the phone talking to Martha in her parlour.

INT. MARTHA'S PARLOUR

Martha is obviously upset by what she is hearing over the phone.   INTERCUT Martha's reactions with John's conversation in his living room.

(s)   SERIES OF SHOTS

As the heading implies, this is a series of short, usually action-type "mini scenes" which serve to move the audience quickly through time or a sequence of events.   Highlights of a sporting event culminating in a "win" for the home team would be an example.   Chase scenes are usually written in this manner.   Each shot is designated with a cap letter.

Example:

SERIES OF SHOTS

A)   CAMERA FOLLOWS Sam Spade running down a shadowy alley.

B)   A car pulls across and blocks the end of the alley.

C)   Sam opens back door of car and runs through as in a Chinese fire drill.

(t)   MONTAGE

Similar to and often confused with a SERIES OF SHOTS,
these two concepts have come to be used interchangeably.   The difference is that a MONTAGE
incorporates more on the screen simultaneously -- at
least two or more different but related subjects which
dissolve in and out of and onto one another.   The
opening scenes of "Apocalypse Now" are an excellent
example of a MONTAGE.   A MONTAGE is stated in the same
way as a SERIES OF SHOTS.

Example:

MONTAGE

A)   AERIAL SHOT - People running wildly through the
       streets

B)   Looting of stores -- people running with armsful
                      of clothing and food

C)   Military police trying to restore order

D)   WIDE SHOT - Planes flying overhead

Notice that, as always, any camera cues are capitalized.
Again, double spacing is used to separate each element
which is designated by a capital letter with close
parenthesis.

NOTE: One of the major differences between a SERIES OF
SHOTS and a MONTAGE is that a SERIES OF SHOTS uses the
principals (the major characters) and is filmed during
the actual shooting schedule of the film.   A MONTAGE is
put together during post production in the editing
process.   Basically a "laboratory" operation if you
will.

EXERCISE FOR TESTING

YOUR KNOWLEDGE OF

SCENE HEADINGS

EXERCISE - A SCENE HEADING ORDER

Listed below are the elements that should appear in a specific scene heading. Arrange these elements in the correct order using correct punctuation and abbreviation. If stage direction information appears in the heading, pull it out and state it as direction.

1. night
    circus train
    full shot
    exterior

2. side show tent
    day
    close on puppet booth
    interior

3. day
    stock
    exterior circus grounds

4. the bearded lady
    e.c.u.

5. medium shot
    the ringmaster and Nick

6. 1974
    day
    exterior the big top

7. montage of circus being
    set up
    elephants holding tent
    poles
    closeup children
    watching wide-eyed
    aerialists practicing
    on high wire

8. the killer lion
    c.u.

9. interior exterior
    day
    ring toss booth

10. establishing
    night
    exterior
    the circus

11. point of view
    near the menagerie
    Billy

12. clock on the wall
    insert
    which reads 8:00

Answer Key on page 45.

EXERCISE KEY

NEXT PAGE

EXERCISE KEY: SCENE HEADINGS

1.   EXT. CIRCUS TRAIN - NIGHT - FULL SHOT

        In this case the camera angle is the last entry.

2.   INT. SIDE SHOW TENT - DAY - CLOSE ON PUPPET BOOTH

        Here, the specific camera subject must be the last entry.

3.   EXT. CIRCUS GROUNDS - DAY - (STOCK)

        Stock is the last entry and must appear in parentheses.

4.   EXTREME CLOSEUP - THE BEARDED LADY

        All camera angles (except MED.) must be spelled out.

5.   MED. SHOT - THE RINGMASTER AND NICK

        Medium shot is the only camera angle that may be
        abbreviated.

6.   EXT. THE BIG TOP - DAY (1974)

        indications of year, time of day and season must appear in
        parentheses.

7.   MONTAGE OF CIRCUS BEING SET UP

        A) Elephants holding tent poles

        B) CLOSEUP of children watching wide-eyed

        C) Aerialists practicing on the high wire

        Elements of a montage must be listed separately, each
        designated with a cap letter and close parenthesis.
        Camera cues must be capitalized.

8.   CLOSEUP - THE KILLER LION

        Camera angle must be spelled out.

9.   INT./EXT. RING TOSS BOOTH - DAY

INT./EXT. is correctly written with a slash indicating a scene that will be shot partially inside and partially outside in a particular area.

10.   EXT. THE CIRCUS - NIGHT - ESTABLISHING

Establishing always appears at the end of the heading but is _not_ placed in parentheses.

11.   BILLY'S POV - NEAR THE MENAGERIE

POV is always abbreviated with no periods. It should be listed after the character whose POV it is. The object of the POV is the last entry.

12.   INSERT - CLOCK ON THE WALL

which reads 8:00.

Detailed information about the INSERT should appear in the stage direction.

HOW TO TAKE A SCENE FROM ONE
PAGE TO ANOTHER

With Scenes Numbered: Use of (CONTINUED)

More often than not, some scenes will continue from one page to the next. The following procedure must be used to continue a scene: At the bottom of the page, the word (CONTINUED) is double spaced down from either direction or dialogue at the bottom of the page and placed on tab (62). (CONTINUED) always appears in caps and parentheses. (See Example 48A opposite)

On the top of the next page the word CONTINUED: appears on line 6 at tab (19). CONTINUED: appears in caps followed by a colon. The continuing scene number (if used) must be restated at margin (13) to give reference to which scene is continuing. (See Example 48B opposite)

Without Scene Numbers

In the event that scene numbers are not assigned, it is not necessary to use scene CONTINUEDS since the term is meaningless without a scene number referral. It is also felt that the absence of the scene CONTINUEDS makes for less clutter in a reading script. On the other hand, there is another school of thought that convincingly argues that the scene CONTINUED will ultimately appear in the script. Therefore, using the CONTINUEDS will give a more accurate page count.

48A - (CONTINUED) - Bottom of Page

---

353   ANGLE - SCARLETT AND RHETT

                         SCARLETT
                       (tearfully)
               Rhet, darling... Come back.
               You know I could not possibly
               be guilty of such a thing.

                                        (CONTINUED)

48B - CONTINUED: - Top of 2nd Page

---

353   CONTINUED:

                         RHETT
               My dear, you give new meaning
               to the word.

HOW TO TAKE A SCENE FROM ONE
PAGE TO ANOTHER

When the scene runs for three or more pages: Use of
CONTINUED:

If a scene continues onto more than two pages (and scene
numbers are used), indicate next to the CONTINUED: at the
top of each page thusly:

132   CONTINUED: (2)

132   CONTINUED: (3)

        and so on.

Remember that it is not necessary to use CONTINUED: (1)
because it is assumed that the first CONTINUED: implies
that this is the first page onto which the material is
continued.

If the scenes are not numbered and CONTINUED is used anyway,
do not used CONTINUED: (2), CONTINUED: (3), etc. Without
scene numbers this information is meaningless.

SO MUCH FOR SCENE HEADINGS...

ON TO SCENE ENDINGS

SCENE ENDINGS

Preliminaries

Scene endings are specific technical instructions indicating the method of moving from one scene to another.

It is assumed that when moving from one scene to the other that we CUT TO: the next scene. Therefore, it is not often necessary to use CUT TO:. Certainly, it is a mistake to mindlessly end every scene in the script with CUT TO: CUT TO: is used for a specific reason: when there is not a logical progression from one scene to the next. For instance if we were at a New York penthouse party, we would CUT TO: the safari camp in the jungle. There are times, however when a more definitive instruction is used to create a certain effect in moving from one scene to another. Again, scene endings should be used sparingly by the writer and with purpose. A scene ending which is a specific technical direction might read: DISSOLVE TO:, CUT TO:, MATCH CUT TO: (See Example 52A opposite)

Format

Scene endings are always capitalized with a colon at tab (62). When the scene ending is too long to fit using tab (62) it must be backed off from the right margin (73). MATCH DISSOLVE TO: is one such case. (See Example 52B opposite)

At The End Of An Act

FADE OUT. is always used as the scene ending at the end of an act. After stating the FADE OUT. double spaced down at tab (62), drop down 6 spaces, center, capitalize and underscore: <u>END OF ACT ONE</u> (or TWO or THREE and so on). (See Example 52C opposite)

At The End Of A Script

FADE OUT. is always used at the end of a script. (This of course necessitates a FADE IN: at the beginning of the script.) In ending a script, FADE OUT. appears double spaced down (from the body), capitalized at tab (62). Spaced down 6, centered, capitalized and underlined appear the words <u>THE END</u>. (See Example 52D opposite)

At All Other Times

When a specific scene ending is used to move out of one scene into another, it is merely a matter of double spacing down and placing the ending on tab (62). It is then necessary to triple space down to the next scene heading since triple spacing is used between scenes.

FADE IN:/FADE OUT./FREEZE FRAME. Rules

FREEZE FRAME. is sometimes incorrectly used as a scene ending. However, it actually works as a camera cue which may be followed by a FADE OUT. Therefore, FREEZE FRAME. is isolated at the left margin and is always followed by a <u>period</u>. (See Example 52D opposite)

FADE OUT. is a scene ending which appears like all others at tab (62) but unlike the others it is punctuated with a period. The logical reason for the period is that FADE OUT. indicates the end of an act or the end of the film. Remember also that FADE OUT. at the end of an act or at the end of a screenplay requires a FADE IN: at the beginning of that act and/or at the beginning of the script. FADE IN:, capitalized, punctuated with a colon, appears at tab (19).

NOTE: FADE OUT. and FADE IN: are sometimes used incorrectly within the body of a screenplay. The correct term to use is FADE TO: which produces the same effect.

52A

DISSOLVE TO:

52B

MATCH DISSOLVE TO:

52C

FADE OUT.

END OF ACT ONE

52D

FREEZE FRAME.

FADE OUT.

THE END

STAGE DIRECTION

Preliminaries

The stage direction, sometimes called the "business" of the scene, is most often referred to as simply direction. It may consist of scene and character descriptions, camera cues, sound cues and various other bits of information needed to facilitate the action, ideas and story line of the script. It is important to note that stage direction need only include the essential information necessary to create the desired effect.

Endless detail and minute descriptions merely create mire through which the reader and production personnnel must wade. Such elaborate detail belongs in novels, not in screenplays where brevity and word economy is essential. The job of technicians, set designers and directors is to utilize their imaginative efforts in tending to such details.

Format

Direction begins at margin [19] and cuts off at [73]. Direction is always double spaced down from the scene heading and extends across the page to the right margin in a single spaced format. Using the cutoff of [73] insures that the direction will not interfere with the scene number on the right side of the page if and when that scene number appears. (See examples opposite)

23   EXT. COTTAGE - DAY   23

      Goldilocks pauses before the neat little cottage
      situated on the edge of the woods. Not knowing what
      to make of it, she moves cautiously up, opens the door
      and peers in.

STAGE DIRECTION: CAPITALIZATION

Know What To Capitalize

Capitalization of words is the means used to spotlight specific technical instructions such as sound and camera cues. Capitalization is also used when a character is first introduced and has a speaking part.

Capitalize Sound Cues

Sound cues are those sounds which require some kind of mechanical production. The sound might be a train whistle off in the distance or a knock on the door. Only the first word indicating a sound need be capitalized since all that is needed is a kind of signpost to alert the sound technician that his efforts are required. (See Examples in 56A opposite)

Often the tendency is to capitalize all the words constituting the sound cue. This practice, while not considered wrong exactly, is nonetheless unnecessary, and may create an unneeded abundance of capitalization in direction.

Spotting Errors

It is important to distinguish between actual sound cues requiring some kind of technical sound effect and those sounds which would be made by the character on the spot. Sounds made by characters are not considered sound cues and do not require capitalization. (See Examples in 56B opposite)

| 56A |

We HEAR the Baskerville Hound baying in the distance.

The lion continues to ROAR menacingly as the two men argue.

The RINGING of the cathedral bells signals death in the village.

| 56B - Not Sound Cues |

Ginger throws the plate to the floor with a crash.

Lionel approaches the door and knocks loudly.

Benny paces beneath the street light, whistling nervously.

STAGE DIRECTION: CAPITALIZATION

Capitalize Camera Cues

Camera instructions and changes often appear in direction. These are considered camera cues for they indicate a specific movement to be carried out by the camera. Therefore, camera cues must always be capitalized to signal the camera operator in the same way that sound cues are capitalized to signal the sound technician. Some camera cues such as CAMERA ZOOMS, CAMERA ADJUSTS, and ANGLE WIDENS TO INCLUDE are obvious and easy to spot. Others, however, are indicated by subtle words such as FOLLOW, SEE, PICK UP, FIND, and so on, and require a keen eye in order that they are not overlooked. (See Example 58A opposite)

Spotting Errors

To help avoid "missing" an obscure camera cue, the reader should think of himself as the camera and may only move when instructed to do so.

58A

CAMERA ZOOMS IN to a CLOSEUP of the secret decoder ring.

CAMERA ADJUSTS to a HIGH ANGLE of the tenement.

ANGLE WIDENS TO INCLUDE Dracula.

We FOLLOW the thief through the crowd.

A moment later we SEE the inspector emerge from a doorway.

The CAMERA FINDS and FOLLOWS Lenore as she breaks away
from the crowd and enters the tomb.

MOVE with the cat burglar as he inches along the ledge.

STAGE DIRECTION: CAPITALIZATION

Cap Character Introductions

When a character is introduced in direction for the first time and
has lines of dialogue, the name is capitalized. This is only done
the first time the character is introduced. After that when he
appears in direction, the name is in upper/lower case.

Understand, however, that capitalization is NOT necessary if the
character is merely mentioned but does not have a speaking part.
He may appear on the screen but if he has no lines, the name is
not capitalized. One can usually tell if a character will have a
speaking part by the amount of detail used in his introductory
description.

Occasionally a "minor character" may not have a speaking role but
may be called upon for significant emotional reaction. In this
and similar cases, it may be appropriate to capitalize the
introduction of that character.

Spotting Errors

Sometimes the characters will not speak immediately after the
introduction but will have lines a few pages later. To be
certain, however, it pays to scan ahead a couple of pages to see
if the character does indeed have lines of dialogue.

60A

INT. THE VANDERBILT HOME/FOYER - NIGHT

The door opens and FELICIA enters with all the drama
of a bowl of raisins. One has great difficulty
getting past the facade, but even those who do are
convinced that it wasn't worth the effort.

                    FELICIA
                (smiling graciously)
          Isn't this a lovely gathering!

60B

The WAITER approaches the table apologetically.

                    WAITER
          I'm dreadfully sorry. We're all
          out of baked jackets.

STAGE DIRECTION: CAPITALIZATION

Cap AD LIB, TITLES, VOICE OVER, BEGIN/END TITLES, FREEZE FRAME.

(a)   AD LIB calls for general, nondescript conversation, laughter, and the like among characters to serve as background atmosphere. AD LIB is always capitalized in direction. (See Example 62A opposite)

(b)   TITLES OF BOOKS, SONGS OR MOVIES sometimes appear in direction and should be capitalized in quotes. Occasionally someone will request that this information appear in upper/lower case and quotes. This would be considered correct as well and should be done as per the author's instructions. The preferred, in most cases, however, is to use caps and quotes. (See Example 62B opposite)

(c)   VOICE OVER when stated in direction must always be capitalized and spelled out. It is never abbreviated in stage direction. (See Example 62C opposite)

(d)   BEGIN TITLES/END TITLES are always capitalized and may appear in direction. It is preferable to isolate these terms (double spaced down) at the margin. In this way it is easy to see at a glance when the film titles should start "rolling" and when they should end. (See Example 62D opposite)

(e)   FREEZE FRAME. works as a camera cue of sorts. Not only is it capitalized, it should be isolated (double spaced down) at the margin, punctuated with a period. (See Example 62E opposite)

62A - AD LIB

Eunice appears in the foyer and the immediate guests AD
LIB comments about her new face lift. AD LIB chatter
floats in from the next room.

62B - Titles Of Books And Songs

The soft music we HEAR is Mancini's theme from "DAYS OF
WINE AND ROSES". Reginald only half listens as he pores
over "CATCHER IN THE RYE".

62C - VOICE OVER

A VOICE OVER muttering is HEARD from the alley.

62D - BEGIN TITLES/END TITLES

AERIAL VIEW - MANHATTAN

depicting the great density of this compact area.

BEGIN TITLES

Slowly PAN DOWN to the helicopter pad on the Pan Am
Building coming to a STOP on a lone figure standing there.

END TITLES.

62E - FREEZE FRAME

Blake finally realizes what has happened, and on his
expression of terror we:

FREEZE FRAME.

                                        FADE OUT.

                        THE END

                         -62-

STAGE DIRECTION: CAPITALIZATION

Notes (To The Director)

On rare occasions, it may be in the interest of clarity to
indicate some technical requirement to give a scene a certain
ambiance or effect. Take heed: This is normally a directorial
consideration which falls to the director who should be able to
conclude what special considerations are required based on the
description and story line of the script. If, however, the writer
feels that a certain technical effect is absolutely necessary, a
note regarding the special consideration may be used.

The correct way to state a note is to move to the left direction
margin, capitalize the word NOTE: followed by a colon. Information in the note itself is in upper/lower case. The entire note
then should be enclosed in parenthesis. The note may fall either
at the beginning or end of the direction, whichever is most
appropriate. (See Example 64A opposite)

Spotting Errors

No Capitalization For Enters and Exits

Whenever it is stated that a character enters or exits a scene,
the words "enters" and "exits" are not capitalized. (See Example
64B opposite)

-63-

64A - Notes To The Director

EXT. TINSELTOWN BAR - NIGHT

There is much AD LIB conversation going on among the patrons.

(NOTE: There should be a lot of glitter used in this scene)

64B - Enters and Exits Are Not Capped

Mildred quickly enters through the side door, drops the paper, and exits through the gallery.

STAGE DIRECTION: ABBREVIATIONS

General Comments

Many words such as personal titles may be abbreviated in direction but cannot be abbreviated in dialogue.   There are a few specific terms that do, in fact, require abbreviation in direction.   These four are:

      1)   f.g. (foreground)

      2)   b.g. (background)

      3)   O.S. (OFF SCREEN)

      4)   M.O.S. (WITHOUT SOUND)*

(See examples opposite)

*M.O.S. is a term as old as talking pictures. Legend has it that a German director ordered a scene to be done "mit out sound." It has been M.O.S. ever since.

Spotting Errors

*(O.S.), off screen, is the correct term used in screenplays or television movies. (O.C.), off camera, is used in taped formats for television (sitcoms, variety shows, etc.)

| 66A |

(a)   In the f.g. we SEE an almost imperceptible movement
        in the grass.

(b)   We HEAR the same creaking sound O.S.

(c)   O.S. there is a fight going on.

(d)   A crowd begins to form in the b.g.

(e)   George and Susan begin talking M.O.S.

        (While we can't hear what they say, there may be
        music or sound effects on the soundtrack)

When Paragraphing Occurs

Although paragraphing in direction is fairly infrequent, whenever
it is necessary, standard paragraphing techniques are used.
It is usually obvious to see where paragraphing should occur,
i.e., to separate the description of a locale from information
regarding the description or action happening in the scene.
Paragraphing, used effectively, can be a creative force.
(See Example 68A opposite)

Breaks in Sentences

Two techniques are used to indicate a pause in a sentence:
the ellipsis (three periods...) or two dashes (--). When
using the ellipsis at the end of a sentence, leave a space
after the third period. When using two dashes leave a space
both before and after the dashes.
(See Example 68B opposite)

Rule for Breaking Direction From One Page to the Next

A passage of direction may be broken from one page to the next
as long as the break comes at the end of a sentence. If the
sentence is long (a writing practice to be avoided in scripts)
the break could conceivable occur after an ellipsis or two
dashes. When direction is broken, it is necessary to use the
scene (CONTINUED) double spaced down at tab 62 with CONTINUED:
stated at the top of the next page.

Use of FLASHBACKS

FLASHBACKS indicate action or events that occurred in a
previous time. This technique must be used ONLY to propel the
story. The FLASHBACK beginning is designated as a scene
isolated at the margin, capitalized and underlined. It is
numbered as a scene. It is also necessary to indicate when
the FLASHBACK ends by merely stating END FLASHBACK isolated at
the margin, capitalized. It is NOT numbered.
(See Example 68C opposite)

68A - Paragraphing

The sun has just begun to set and there is a mist
hovering in the valley below.

Juan stands fixed and unmoving on the ledge overlooking
the scene. There is no sign of the pack-horses.

He turns slowly and we SEE the anguish on his face.

68B - Breaks in Sentences

Marguerite slowly sweeps the curtain aside and gazes
wistfully out -- will he keep his promise?

The rider on the horse tentatively approaches the fork
in the road and hesitates. Is it the road to the
north? Or the road to the east? The decision is
crucial, for if he takes the wrong road... His look
says it all.

68C - FLASHBACKS

FLASHBACK - BERLIN (1943)

A boy of ten stands bewildered and confused amid
exploding shells and burning buildings. A German
soldier runs to him.

                    SOLDIER
          Come! I know a safe place.

END FLASHBACK

COMPOSITE: STAGE DIRECTION

What follows on the page opposite is a composite example incorporating the major considerations just discussed in stage direction.

Each element to be considered is numbered with the number corresponding to the explanation which is below the composite. Listed also is the page number on which the original text information appears.

EXT. FOREST - DAY (SPRINGTIME)

(NOTE: Use a filter for this scene.) (1)

A purple twilight is slowly moving over this lush
forest primeval. (2) We HEAR (3) Tiny Tim's version
of "TIPTOE THROUGH THE TULIPS" (4) in the b.g. (5)
as the CAMERA PICKS UP (6) Red Riding Hood who enters
(7) the scene skipping merrily. FOLLOW (8) her as
she glides down the path and then stops to pick a
nosegay of wild flowers. Suddenly there is the O.S.
(9) SOUND (10) of a twig breaking. Red Riding Hood
looks up and listens to a low, deep, VOICE OVER
GROANING, (11 & 12), emanating from the bushes in the
f.g. (13). PULL BACK (14) to reveal THE WOLF (15)
grumbling AD LIB (16) curses about a thorn in his
paw.

Explanation:

(1)	Note to the director (Pg. 63)
(2)	Standard paragraphing (Pg. 67)
(3)	Sound cue, capped (Pg. 55)
(4)	Song title, capped in quotes (Pg. 61)
(5)	Background, lower case, abbreviated (Pg. 65)
(6)	Camera cue, capped (Pg. 57)
(7)	Enters/exits, not capped (Pg. 63)
(8)	Camera cue, capped (Pg. 57)
(9)	Off Screen, capped, upper case, abbreviated (Pg. 65)
(10)	Sound cue, capped, (Pg. 55)
(11)	VOICE OVER, always capped (Pg. 61)
(12)	Sound cue, capped (Pg. 55)
(13)	Foreground, lower case, abbreviated (Pg. 65)
(14)	Camera cue, capped (Pg. 57)
(15)	Character introduction, capped (Pg. 59)
(16)	AD LIB, capped (Pg. 61)

EXERCISE: STAGE DIRECTION

Circle the words that should be capitalized, abbreviated, and/or punctuated in the following passage of direction.

EXT. HAUNTED HOUSE - NIGHT

Occasional lightning flickers in the background and we hear the sound of thunder periodically.

The camera pulls back to include the two boys. A variety of "ghostly" sounds emanate from the house causing the boys to crouch lower beneath the windowsill. They ad lib their fears in nervous whispers. We hear the ominious musical strains of The Sorcerer's Apprentice. Suddenly over a P.A. system, the voice over laughter of the legendary witch permeates the entire house. The boys quickly turn at the o.s. sound of leaves crunching beneath slowly advancing footsteps.

                    WITCH (O.S.)
          Stay where you are, my lovelies!

EXERCISE KEY

NEXT PAGE

EXT. HAUNTED HOUSE - NIGHT

Occasional lightning flickers in the b.g. and we HEAR
the sound of thunder periodically.

The CAMERA PULLS BACK to INCLUDE the two boys. A
variety of "ghostly" SOUNDS emanate from the house
causing the boys to crouch lower beneath the
windowsill. They AD LIB their fears in nervous
whispers. We HEAR the ominious musical strains of
"THE SORCERER'S APPRENTICE." Suddenly over a P.A.
system, the VOICE OVER LAUGHTER of the legendary witch
permeates the entire house. The boys quickly turn at
the O.S. SOUND of leaves crunching beneath slowly
advancing footsteps.

                    WITCH (O.S.)
          Stay where you are, my lovelies!

CHARACTER CUES

Preliminaries

The character cue is simply the name of the character to whom lines of dialogue are assigned. Usually the character is designated by either the first or last name. A role designation may be used for small parts where the character is not given a name. Whether using first or last name in character cue, keep the reference consistent throughout the script. (See Example 76A opposite)

Format Rules

The character cue is always stated in capital letters at typewriter tab 43. The first letter of the character name should fall in the vertical center of the page when folded lengthwise.

Abbreviate Personal Titles

Personal titles are usually abbreviated in the character cue. It's important to keep the character cue short and succinct to be easily read. (See Example 76B opposite)

Use of (V.O.) and (O.S.)

(V.O.) or VOICE OVER means that the character is usually not seen on screen but we hear his voice conveyed over some kind of mechanical contrivance such as a telephone or tape recorder. In the opening scene of the old "Rockford Files" series, we hear his VOICE OVER on the answering machine. There may be a scene requiring narration which will be (V.O.). Here the character might be thinking out loud. We hear the voice (recorded on tape in post production after the filming is completed) while the camera is on him. When a character is talking on the other end of the telephone and does not appear on camera it's a VOICE OVER situation. (See Example 76C opposite)

(O.S.) or OFF SCREEN/OFF STAGE means that the character is not seen on screen but we hear him talking from another room in a house or some adjacent area. In an (O.S.) situation the character is readily available to appear on camera. Both (V.O.) and (O.S.) are capitalized in parentheses, abbreviated with periods, next to the character name. (See Example 76C opposite)

76A - Specific Role as a Character Cue

SAILOR

POLICEMAN

CLOWN

76B - Abbreviation of Personal Titles

COL. SANDERS

CAPT. CRUNCH

DR. JEKYLL

76C - (V.O.) and (O.S.)

ALEXANDER GRAHAM BELL (V.O.)

JACK THE RIPPER (O.S.)

CHARACTER CUES

Specific Roles Are Placed In Parentheses

The specific role of a character may be designated in the
character cue along with the character name. This information
should appear capitalized in parentheses beside the character
cue. (See Example 78A opposite)

No Name Cue

The character cue may only be a role designation without the
name. (See Example 78B opposite)

Use Of Numbers

If there is more than one character playing the same role, it
should be designated by using #1, #2, and so on after the role.
(See Example 78C opposite)

78A - Character Cue With Role Designation

JONATHAN (NARRATOR)

THOMAS (JESTER)

ANSEL ADAMS (PHOTOGRAPHER)

78B - Role Designation As Character Cue

BYSTANDER

WAITRESS

REPORTER

78C - Several Characters In The Same Role

LILLIPUTIAN #1

DECK HAND #3

ROBOT #5

CHARACTER CUES

Consistency

Spotting Errors

Consistency in the character cue thoughout the script is important. The author may start out calling the character by the first name and then switch to using the last name throughout the rest of the script. While it does not matter how the character is referred to -- either by the first name or the last -- the name should be stated consistently throughout the script.

NOTES

PERSONAL DIRECTION

Preliminaries

Personal direction, which should be used sparingly, consists of those special, usually short instructions intended for a specific character and no one else. These instructions might include: (sits down), (laughs evilly), (stops, wipes brow), (continuing), (beat), (pauses) and the like. Remember that both (beat) and (continuing) are personal direction along with (sotto) or (sotto voce). Here also is where to indicate that the dialogue should be delivered with a particular accent or in fact should be spoken in another language. (See Example 82D, 82E opposite)

Format

Personal direction always appears directly under the character cue, in parentheses, at tab (36) and cuts off at tab (55) -- approximately 19 characters (letters and spaces) long. All words are in lower case...

(See Incorrect Example 82A and Correct Example 82B opposite)

...except those words which would normally be capitalized such as proper nouns. (See Correct Example 82C opposite)

Notice also that the second line and all subsequent lines are indented one space so that the first letter of the line does not fall directly under the parenthesis. (See Example 82C opposite)

Personal direction may occur more than once in a given segment of dialogue but the basic rules are the same throughout. (See Example 82D opposite)

82A - Incorrect

                    HOLMES
                (Leaning forward)

82B - Correct

                    HOLMES
                (leaning forward)

82C - Correct

                    HOLMES
                (holding the note,
                 moving toward
                 Moriarty)

82D - Correct

                    WATSON
                (uncertain)
        I think...
                (beat)
        Miss Adler, that's who it was.

82E - Correct

                    HOLMES
                (sotto)
        Just as I thought.
                (excitedly)
        Come along, Watson. We're off to
        Liverpool!

PERSONAL DIRECTION

How To "Pull Out" Long Passages Of Personal Direction

Personal direction should be no more than four lines long. If it turns out to be longer, it must be "pulled out" to the margin and stated as stage direction. When doing so, however, the character name may have to be re-stated in that direction for clarity's sake. The tense of words may also have to be altered in order that the direction makes sense. (See Incorrect Example 84A and Correct Example 84B opposite)

Spotting Errors

Personal Direction Under the Wrong Cue: If another character's personal direction is mistakenly placed under a given character cue, that personal direction belonging to another character must be "pulled out" to the margin to become stage direction. (See Incorrect Example 84C and Correct Example 84D opposite)

NOTE: In spotting personal direction placed under the wrong character cue, it may help to visualize the character cue, personal direction, and dialogue in a box in the center of the page. Everything in this imaginary box belongs to that one character: His character cue, his personal direction, his dialogue. Nothing else may appear here.

84A - Long Passages - Incorrect

                              HOLMES
                         (thoughtfully
                          puffing on his
                          calabash, pacing
                          back and forth
                          in front of the
                          window)

84B - Long Passages - Correct

Holmes, thoughtfully puffing on his calabash, paces back
and forth in front of the window.

84C - Personal Direction - Incorrect

                              HOLMES
                         (to Watson in
                          next room)
                    I think I have it, Watson. Come
                    take a look at this.
                         (Watson enters)
                    The clay from his boots is red in
                    colour like that found on the
                    Sussex Moors.

84D - Personal Direction - Correct

                              HOLMES
                         (to Watson in
                          next room)
                    I think I have it, Watson. Come
                    take a look at this.

Watson enters.

                              HOLMES
                         (continuing)
                    The clay from his boots is red in
                    colour like that found on the
                    Sussex Moors.

PERSONAL DIRECTION

Rule: Don't End a Page With Personal Direction

When breaking dialogue from one page to the next, the break must
fall before the personal (parenthetical) direction. The personal
direction must then be placed on the next page rather than leaving
it "dangle" at the bottom of the preceding page. (See incorrect
Example 86A and Correct Example 86B opposite)

In general, personal direction should never end a passage of
dialogue. Even if the direction is only a word or two, it is best
to pull it out to the stage direction margin.

86A - Incorrect

22.

> HOLMES
> From my analysis of this ash, we
> are dealing with a rare cigar...
> imported.
> > (beat)
> > > (MORE)

(CONTINUED)

23.

CONTINUED:

> HOLMES (CONT'D)
> Come, Watson. The game's afoot!

- -

86B - Correct

22.

> HOLMES
> From my analysis of this ash, we
> are dealing with a rare cigar...
> imported.
> > (MORE)

(CONTINUED)

23.

CONTINUED:

> HOLMES (CONT'D)
> > (beat)
> Come, Watson.   The game's afoot!

DIALOGUE: RULES

Preliminaries

Since the words uttered by a character are often the vehicle by which a production "moves", it stands to reason that those words are extremely important. Dialogue is, in a word, sacred. When typing scripts for someone else it's essential to realize that dialogue should not be changed or altered without consultation with the writer or other individuals in charge.

Format

The format and rules that apply to dialogue are formulated to aid clarity and conciseness. Visually, the lines spoken by a given character in a script are obvious for they are located in the center of the page and are relatively short. Dialogue begins at tab (29) and cuts off at tab (60). Upper/lower case is used. Again, dialogue along with the character cue and personal direction, falls within an imaginary box in the middle of the page. (See Example 88A opposite)

88A - Visual Placement of Dialogue

17   EXT. GARDEN AREA - DAY

    Mr. McGregor is having an animated conversation with Peter.

                    MR. McGREGOR
          What are you doing in this
          garden? Explain yourself.

                    PETER
          Well, let's just say that I'm
          heavy into produce.

                    MR. McGREGOR
          I'm heavy into produce as well,
          but from a different point of
          view.

                    PETER
          Rather seems like a case of supply
          and demand, doesn't it?

                    MR. McGREGOR
          So it would seem. My supply and
          your demand.

DIALOGUE: RULES

Follow Precise Spelling and Grammatical Rules

Most of the following rules can also be found in Appendix B called "Universal Truths". Many of these rules are those of standard grammar, while others concern those special considerations peculiar to dialogue.

(a)   Spell out:

            1)   One and two digit numbers. (Three or more digits
                    may be written numerically.)

            2)   Personal titles, except for Mr., Mrs., and Ms.
                    which may be abbreviated.

            3)   Indications of time. Example: one-thirty.

            4)   Okay, and all other words it might be tempting to
                    abbreviate such as doctor. When in doubt, spell
                    it out.

(b)   No Hyphenation

            Words may not be hyphenated from one line to the next.
            Those words which are normally hyphenated may be
            extended to the next line. Example: son-in-law.

(c)   Never break a sentence from one page to the next. End
            the sentence before moving to the next page.

(d)   Pauses in a sentence may be indicated with the ellipsis
            (three periods). A space should be left after the third
            period. (See Example 90A opposite)

(e)   The ellipsis is also used when a sentence is interrupted
            by personal direction. In this case, the ellipsis must
            appear both at the end break and at the beginning of the
            remainder of the sentence. (See Example 90B opposite)

(f)   Pauses may also be indicated by using two dashes. Leave
            a space on each side of them.   (See Example 90C
            opposite)

(g)   Paragraphing may be used in long passages of dialogue
            but the practice is rare. Usually personal direction is
            used to indicate a change of thought.

90A - The Ellipsis as a Pause

                    STANLEY
          He may not even be... alive.

90B - The Ellipsis with Personal Direction Interruption

                    STANLEY
          Trying to find him in all this...
                    (gestures)
          ... sometimes seems so futile.

90C - Dashes Used as a Pause

                    STANLEY
          We must press on -- at all costs.

DIALOGUE: BREAKING DIALOGUE

Breaking Dialogue: When To Use (MORE)

When a character has a lengthy dialogue which must be continued
onto the next page, the dialogue must be broken at the end of a
sentence. (If it's a stream of consciousness speech with no
punctuation other than ellipses or dashes, then the break should
be made at the pause.) To indicate broken dialogue, use the word
(MORE). The term (MORE) applies to dialogue and only to dialogue.

(a)   Format Rules

       1)   (MORE) always appears capitalized in parentheses,
                 single spaced down from the last sentence of
                 dialogue.

       2)   (MORE) is logically stated at the character cue
                 tab 43 since it is the character who has more
                 lines. (See Example 92A opposite)

       NOTE: Remember that when dialogue continues it
       automatically means that the scene is (CONTINUED) as well.

How To Use (CONT'D)

After stating (MORE) to indicate more dialogue, on the next page
the term (CONT'D)* must be stated after the character cue. (See
Example 92B opposite)

(a)   Format Rules

       1)   (CONT'D) alwys appears in upper case and
                 parentheses, abbreviated.

       2)   (CONT'D) always appears beside the character cue.

       NOTE: Remember that the scene CONTINUED: must be stated on
       the next page (if scene numbers are used). (See Example 92B
       opposite)

* It has been previously advised that (CONT'D) be stated in upper
and lower case. However, usage has evolved the upper case version
since the character cue is always capitalized.

92A - Use Of (MORE)

4.

8   CONTINUED:

                    RED RIDING HOOD
          My grandmother is feeling quite
          poorly... she lives just beyond
          the woods... and I'm taking her a
          food basket.
                  (MORE)

                            (CONTINUED)

92B - Use Of (CONT'D)

5.

8   CONTINUED: (2)

                    RED RIDING HOOD (CONT'D)
          I must hurry now before the soup
          gets cold.

DIALOGUE: BREAKING DIALOGUE
_____

(a)   (continuing) after stage direction in the middle of the
        page.

        There are times when a character's dialogue is interrupted
        by stage direction. When this occurs, the character cue
        must be restated after the direction with (continuing),
        single spaced underneath in parentheses at [personal
        direction] tab (36). (See Example 94A opposite)

(b)   (continuing) after stage direction at the bottom of the
        page.

        When the character's dialogue is interrupted by stage
        direction, and that direction happens to fall at the bottom
        of the page, the character cue must be restated on the next
        page as (continuing) in the same format as stated above.
        (See Example 94B opposite)

        NOTE: (continuing) is used to continue a character's
        dialogue regardless of where that dialogue is interrupted by
        stage direction. Even if the direction at the bottom of the
        page in Example 94B were to be placed on the top of the next
        page... which is optional depending on space, the use of
        continuing is still the same. The scene is (CONTINUED) at
        the bottom of the page and and again CONTINUED: at the top
        of the next page. After the direction is stated, the
        character is restated as before with (continuing).

```
| 94A - Stage Direction Interrupting Dialogue, Middle of Page |
```

                    GUINEVERE
          Will you return for the jousting
          tournament?

     Arthur looks up with concern.

                    GUINEVERE
                   (continuing)
          It would be important to your
          people to see you there.

```
| 94B - Stage Direction Interrupting, Bottom of Page |
```

                    GUINEVERE
          Will you return for the jousting
          tournament?

     Arthur looks up with concern.

                                        (CONTINUED)

_____

(new page)

23   CONTINUED:

                    GUINEVERE
                   (continuing)
          It would be important to your
          people to see you there.

DIALOGUE: BREAKIING DIALOGUE

How (continuing) And (beat) Are Related

(c)   (continuing) and (beat) used with personal direction.

       When (continuing) or (beat) is used along with other
       personal direction, a semicolon must be used to separate
       them from the rest of the personal direction. (See Example
       96A opposite)

(d)   When (continuing) is not necessary.

       It is not necessary to use (continuing) when a character's
       dialogue shifts from a (V.O.) situation to live dialogue.
       It is infrequent that this would ever happen but when it
       does, the thinking is that the (V.O.) dialogue and the live
       dialogue are considered two different entities, so there is
       not really any continuation. (See Example 96b opposite)

96A - (continuing) And (beat) Used With Personal Direction

                    WATSON
               (continuing;
                sheepishly)

or

                    WATSON
               (beat; to Holmes)

or

                    WATSON
               (continuing; beat)

96B - Going From (V.O.) To Live Dialogue

    Holmes stares at the fire pondering the day's events.

                    HOLMES (V.O.)
          I know there was some connection
          between the two men. I wonder if
          they remembered that I knew them
          fifteen years ago in Manchester.
          I wonder if...

                    HOLMES
          Watson, pull out your file on
          "The Blue Carbuckle".

What follows is a composite example of
several screenplay pages. These sample
pages are in correct standard format
and incorporate most of the elements of
information previously discussed.

SABOTAGE

FADE IN:

1   EXT. LOS ANGELES - DAY   1

It is an incredibly clear afternoon as our CAMERA PANS
the Los Angeles basin and ZOOMS IN on a specific
structure in the Wilshire District.

TITLES BEGIN

As we reach the structure, the SOUNDS of the city
become prominent.

                                              CUT TO:

2   EXT. OFFICE BUILDING - DAY - CLOSE ANGLE - ENTRANCE   2

People are returning from their lunch hour breaks --
lots of street traffic. Finally, a taxi pulls up and
we PICK UP the occupant as he exits the cab. This is
ALEX MILLS, a very handsome, athletic type, mid-
thirties and very aggressive. As he closes the cab
door he drops a newspaper.

3   INSERT - NEWSPAPER   3

Headline reads, "MILLS INJUNCTION IMMINENT".

                                        MATCH DISSOLVE TO:

4   INT. OFFICE - DAY - ON NEWSPAPER HEADLINE   4

as it is being picked up from a desk. CAMERA ADJUSTS
to include Alex entering from outer office. We cannot
see who is holding the paper, we only HEAR a voice:

                    VOICE (O.S.)
            Alex, my dear boy... have you seen
            this morning's rag?

                    ALEX
                (very calm)
            Of course, Father -- and I know
            what you're going to say.
                    (MORE)

                                              (CONTINUED)

4   CONTINUED: 4

                          ALEX (CONT'D)
                "Why are you doing this to
                me..." Right?
                          (slumps down in
                           a chair)
                the "why" should be apparent --
                but... I expected this reaction
                from you.

5   CLOSE SHOT - ALEXANDER MILLS SR.   5

a somewhat staunch-looking business executive type in
his late sixties. At the moment he is at a loss for
words. Evidently he is overwhelmed by the story in the
newspaper he is clutching.

END TITLES.

6   MED. TWO SHOT - ALEX AND MILLS SR.   6

                          MILLS SR.
                Alex, so help me... if this goes
                to court I will hold you
                personally responsible!

7   EXTREME CLOSEUP - ALEX   7

Words cannot convey the contempt we see in his face as
we:

                                              FADE TO:

8   EXT. LOS ANGELES STREET - DAY - ESTABLISHING   8

9   EXT./INT. BAR - DAY   9

We are ON a sign which reads: "CANDY'S". We PAN DOWN
to the entrance and PICK UP and FOLLOW Alex as he
enters the bar. It is dimly lit and only a handful of
people are scattered about. There is no AD LIB
conversation in the b.g.

10   ALEX'S POV - GLORIA   10

sitting alone, inhaling on a cigarette. She's a
stylish woman inher early thirties... one of those
people who always has everything under control.

11   ANGLE ON ALEX   11

as he moves toward Gloria.

> ALEX
> (exhilarated)
> Gloria, it's working. It's really
> working!

Gloria can only control her emotion for a few short
beats and then the slightest smile crosses her face.

> ALEX
> (continuing)
> Well... tell me what you're
> thinking.

DISSOLVE TO:

12   SERIES OF SHOTS - M.O.S.   12

A) Gloria and Mills Sr. having dinner together in a
quaint little dinner club.

B) FULL SHOT - An usher seating them in a theater.

CLOSE SHOT - Gloria and Mills Sr. in a long kiss before
CAMERA PULLS BACK to reveal they are in front of her
apartment building.

CUT TO:

13   INT. ALEX'S LIVING ROOM - NIGHT   13

Alex is dressed in a bathrobe, lounging with a drink in
hand. A sudden impulse and he picks up the phone and
begins dialing.

14   INTERCUT - GLORIA'S BEDROOM - CLOSE ON PHONE   14

as it begins to RING. PULL BACK to SEE Gloria enter
from the adjoining bathroom. She quickly picks up the
receiver.

> GLORIA
> Hello...

> ALEX
> Gloria, I had to call. Something
> has been bothering me all evening.

SMASH CUT TO:

15   HIGH ANGLE - HELICOPTER POV - BURNING BUILDING   15

We SEE the smouldering and charred remains of what
appears to have been a warehouse. The end of a
newscast FADES UP:

                    ANNOUNCER (V.O.)
          Authorities say that they have not
          yet determined the cause of the
          fire...

16   CLOSE ANGLE   16

The wisps of smoke that remain only partially obscure a
sign which reads: "MILLS MANUFACTURING".

                                        FADE OUT.

                    THE END

The next four pages are an example of standard shooting script format. Following is the same example only in reading form. Beginning writers will want to use the reading form when submitting a project to an agent.

"RIOT!"

FADE IN:

1   EXT. LOS ANGELES, 1968 - AERIAL SHOT - DAY

A panoramic view of familiar Los Angeles sites: The
Hollywood Bowl, Hollywood and Vine, the Capitol Records
Building, a freeway, downtown area. Finally ZOOM IN to:

2   EXT. WATTS - ESTABLISHING SHOT

A small crowd of blacks gathered around a police car.
Two officers, one white, one black, are attempting to
control the crowd. The black officer, SGT. EDWARDS,
about 40, is a veteran policeman who goes strictly by
"the book" but yet tries to remain a "brother" and
speak their language.

                    EDWARDS
          Okay, everybody, cool it! Go on
          about your business.

The other officer, BROOKS, a brash, young rookie, is
holding a black youth by the arm. His name is LESTER.

                    LESTER
           (to crowd)
          This white pig pushed me, man.
          Nobody gonna push me aroun'.

CAMERA PANS the crowd as they react with AD LIBS:
"Yeah!" "You tell 'em, brother!" The crowd is growing
now, getting noisier. The mood is intense. Years of
anger seem to be surfacing all at once. CAMERA PAN
ENDS on:

                    BROOKS
           (meaning Lester)
          We have several warrants for this
          man's arrest. Now he's resisting!

3   BROOKS' POV - THE CROWD

They are moving forward, menacingly.

4   BACK TO SCENE

Edwards moves to the police car and picks up the car
mike to radio for assistance.

                              (CONTINUED)

4   CONTINUED:

Several blacks begin pushing the police car swinging it
back and forth. The crowd now is much larger. They
are yelling and cursing. The CAMERA MOVES IN on their
angry faces as we:

                                          DISSOLVE TO:

5   INT./EXT. APPLIANCE STORE - NIGHT - CLOSE ON STORE OWNER

who is being tied up by two blacks. CAMERA WIDENS and
we SEE several blacks milling around, taking toasters,
irons, and whatever they can carry. We can HEAR the
rioting noises O.S. One black man, laden with loot,
hurriedly walks toward an exit and out of the building.

Outside, the riot is in full swing.

6   SERIES OF SHOTS

     A) Looters break store windows.

     B) Blacks setting a building on fire.

     C) A cop car, overturned, its windows broken.

                                          CUT TO:

7   EXT. ROADBLOCK - NIGHT - MED. SHOT

Several police cars, lights flashing, are parked close
together. Helmeted police helplessly watch the rioters
in the distance. MOVE IN on TWO POLICEMEN. They are
drinking coffee from paper cups.

                    POLICEMAN #1
          I've never seen anything like it.
          On the force 22 years.

The other Policeman nods in agreement as he leans
uncomfortably against the squad car.

                    POLICEMAN #2
          Have you ever shot anybody?

They are interrupted by the VOICE OVER car radio.

                                          (CONTINUED)

7   CONTINUED:

> VOICE OVER (CONT'D)
> (filtered)
> Helicopter Ten-Z calling Roadblock-
> A. A large crowd is gathering at
> Fifty-Fourth Street and Western
> Avenue. They are carrying what
> appear to be Molotov cocktails.
> (beat)
> There are 500 National Guardsmen due
> to arrive at 10:00 p.m.

8   INT. KITCHEN - SEVERAL DAYS LATER

MR. ATKINS is sitting at the kitchen table with his
daughter, HELEN. His 72 years in Watts have given him
the patience and wisdom the younger generation lacks.
In the b.g. his grandchildren are playing.

> ATKINS
> I tole that husband of yours to
> stay home but he wouldn't listen.

> HELEN
> He'll be all right...

> ATKINS
> I've never seen anything like it.
> I'm glad your ma wasn't here to
> witness this.
> (beat)
> Ain't no good gonna come to our
> people.

Helen goes to stove to get coffee pot.

> ATKINS
> (continuing)
> What're we gonna do?

> JAMES (O.S.)
> (calling)
> Helen! Poppa!

JAMES walks into the kitchen carrying a television set.

> JAMES
> Look what I got, Poppa!

> ATKINS
> What you got there, boy?

(CONTINUED)

8   CONTINUED:

INTERCUT children's reaction to their grandpa's anger.

                    ATKINS
          I don't want no stolen merchandise
          in my house.

                    JAMES
          Everybody's doing it, Poppa.
          There's stuff just sittin' all
          over the sidewalk.

We can HEAR people shouting and running O.S.

                    VOICE (O.S.)
          Here come the pigs again!

                    ATKINS
          Listen to them. Haven't you
          learned anything from this, James?

                    JAMES
          Yeah... I learned how you get
          folks to hear you. Nobody listens
          when you talk soft.

                    ATKINS
          What good's gonna come of wreckin'
          our own schools and destroyin'
          property?

                    JAMES
          Our people are sick of talk.
          We're sick of askin' for handouts.
          Only one thing those suckers
          understan'. We had to act. It
          was the only way.

9   CLOSE SHOT - MR. ATKINS

His look reflects deep, troubled concern. Slowly he
turns his gaze to the children who have stopped playing
and are now listening and wondering.

RIOT!

FADE IN:

EXT. LOS ANGELES, 1968 - DAY

The panoramic view of Los Angeles is dazzling. Familiar
sites are a reminder of how exciting this city is. The
Hollywood Bowl, Hollywood and Vine, the Capitol Records
Building, a freeway, downtown L.A. But there are other
sites less familiar and less dazzling.

EXT. WATTS - DAY

A small crowd of blacks are gathered around a police
car. Two officers, one white, one black, are
attempting to control the crowd. The black officer,
Sgt. Edwards, about 40, is a veteran policeman who goes
strictly by "the book" yet tries to remain a "brother"
and speak their language.

> EDWARDS
> Okay, everybody, cool it! Go on
> about your business.

The other officer, Brooks, a brash, young rookie, is
holding a black youth by the arm. His name is LESTER.

> LESTER
> (to crowd)
> This white pig pushed me, man.
> Nobody gonna push me aroun'.

Angry faces in the crowd react shouting "Yeah!" "You
tell 'em, brother!" The group is growing in both
numbers and volume. Faces intense. Mood volatile.
Years of disillusionment and frustration seem to be
surfacing all at once.

> BROOKS
> (meaning Lester)
> We have several warrants for this
> man's arrest. Now he's resisting!

The crowd moves forward, menacingly.

Edwards moves to the police car and picks up the car
mike to radio for assistance.

Several blacks begin pushing the police car swinging it back and forth. Their numbers still more than before. Their faces distorted with anger.

INT. APPLIANCE STORE - NIGT

The terrified owner is being tied up by two blacks. Several other blacks are milling around taking toasters, irons, and whatever else they can carry.

The rioting noises continue. One black man, laden with loot, hurriedly walks toward an exit and out of the building.

OUTSIDE

It's a war zone. Looters breaking store windows, fire set to a building, an overturned cop car, the windows broken out.

EXT. ROADBLOCK - NIGHT

Several police cars, lights flashing, are parked close together. Helmeted police helplessly watch the rioters in the distance. Two policemen are drinking coffee from paper cups.

                    POLICEMAN #1
          I've never seen anything like it.
          On the force 22 years.

The other Policeman nods in agreement as he leans uncomfortably against the squad car.

                    POLICEMAN #2
          Have you ever shot anybody?

They are interrupted by a voice on the car radio.

                    VOICE ON RADIO
          Helicopter Ten-Z calling Roadblock
          A. A large crowd is gathering at
          Fifty-Fourth Street and Western
          Avenue. They are carrying what
          appear to be Molotov cocktails.
                    (MORE)

                    VOICE ON RADIO (CONT'D)
               (beat)
          There are 500 National Guardsmen
          due to arrive at 10:00 p.m.

INT. KITCHEN - SEVERAL DAYS LATER

Mr. Atkins is sitting at the kitchen table with his
daughter, Helen. His 72 years in Watts have given him
the patience and wisdom the younger generation lacks.
His grandchildren play in the background.

                    ATKINS
          I tol' that husband of yours to
          stay home but he wouldn't listen.

                    HELEN
          He'll be all right...

                    ATKINS
          I've never seen anything like it.
          I'm glad your ma wasn't here to
          witness this.
               (beat)
          Ain't no good gonna come to our
          people.

Helen goes to the stove to get the coffee pot.

                    ATKINS
          What're we gonna do?

                    JAMES
               (calling)
          Helen! Poppa!

James walks into the kitchen carrying a television set.

                    JAMES
          Look what I got, Poppa!

                    ATKINS
          What you got there, boy?

During this conversation we notice the children's
startled reaction to their grandpa's anger.

                    ATKINS
          I don't want no stolen merchandise
          in my house.

> JAMES
> Everybody's doing it, Poppa.
> There's stuff just sittin' all over
> the sidewalk.

Outside people are shouting and running. "Here come the pigs
again!"

> ATKINS
> Listen to them. Haven't you
> learned anything from this, James?

> JAMES
> Yeah... I learned how you get folks
> to hear you. <u>Nobody</u> listens when
> you talk soft.

> ATKINS
> What good's gonna come of wreckin'
> our own schools and destroyin'
> property?

> JAMES
> Our people are sick of talk. We're
> sick of askin' for handouts. Only
> one thing those suckers understan'.
> We had to act. It was the only way.

Mr. Atkins' face reflects deep, troubled concern.
Slowly he turns his gaze to the children who have
stopped playing and are now listening and wondering.

THE FILM IN PRODUCTION

When a film finally gets to the point that it goes into production, changes in the script inevitably occur. Sometimes there are major rewrites and other times only subtle changes are made. The pages on which the changes occur become revision pages. If there are extensive changes, the script may be re-written as a Revised Draft or a Revised Final Draft.

The draft of a script usually indicates how often there have been rewrites. There may be a First Draft, a Second Draft, sometimes a Third Draft, a Final Draft, and so on. When things get really desperate and there are no more names to call them, we have known production companies to use such nomenclature as "Root Beer Draft" and "No Kidding, This Is It Draft". The latter are by no means standard or even accepted in some circles but do serve to illustrate numerous, imaginative possibilities!

HOW TO HANDLE REVISION PAGES

Revision Pages Are Color Coded

Whenever material in the script is re-written, deleted, or added, these changes become revision pages. Revision pages scattered throughout the script are color coded to designate how many times changes were made. The color coded change progression works as follows:

                    1st Revision -- Blue
                    2nd Revision -- Pink
                    3rd Revision -- Yellow
                    4th Revision -- Green
                    5th Revision -- Gold
                    6th Revision -- Back to White

In this way, one can tell at a glance which pages have been changed and how many times changes have occurred.

<u>REVISION PAGES</u>

Always "Hold" Page and Scene Numbers

(a)   All Page and Scene Numbers Must Be Accounted For.

Page and scene numbers on revision pages must always be "held" or kept the same as they appear on the original copy of the script. In this way, the newly changed page can be inserted in the existing scripts and the numbering will still flow consecutively. In effect, revisions are done page for page. The main consideration is that all pages and scenes must be accounted for... both <u>additions and deletions</u>.

(b)   What Are "A" Pages?

There are times when the material will not all fit on a given page and may extend onto an additional page or pages. In this case "A" pages are used. The original page number is retained, and all subsequent pages use capital letters along with the page number. The page numbers then might run 7., 7A., 7B., 7C., 8. There may or may not be the requirement of placing asterisks after the page number to indicate that the page has been added or changed for the most part. (See page 129: Revision Exercise Key)

(c)   What Are "Runs"?

If, on the other hand, there are several consecutive pages from which material has been omitted, this sequence of pages is known as a run. The procedure for handling a run is to "tighten" it up, that is, type full pages all the way through to the last page in the sequence and then make a "combination" page at the end. Depending on the amount of material omitted one or more pages might be "lost". The page numbers would then appear: page 9/10. (using a slash if two or more pages combined into one page). Or 7-10. (using a dash if three or more pages combine into one page). This technique is used to indicate that pages or large sections of material have been deleted. (See page 132: Revision Exercise Key)

How To Add Or Omit Scenes

Handling scene numbers on revision pages involves the same basic procedure as page numbers in that "A" scenes are used when additional scenes have been added. (See Example 114A opposite) When a scene is deleted, it must be stated as "OMITTED" (See Example 114B opposite)

Spotting Errors

Notice that if <u>two consecutive</u> scenes are OMITTED, the word AND should appear between the scene numbers on the left and on the right side. (See Example 114C opposite) If <u>three or more</u> consecutive scenes are OMITTED, the word THRU should appear between the scene numbers instead of the word AND. (See Example 114D opposite)

114A - Scene Additions Or "A" Scenes

277   277

277A   277A

277B   277B

278   278

114B - Scene Omits

276   OMITTED   276

114C

278   OMITTED   278
AND   AND
279   279

114D

278   OMITTED   278
THRU   THRU
281   281

REVISION PAGES: HEADINGS

Headings On Revisions Vary According to Production Needs

Revision pages nearly always carry a heading which may include
some or all of the following information: Title of script or
episode title (if a television series), the word Rev. and the
current date stated in numbers. The production company dictates
what it requires in the heading. Frequently only the word Rev.
and the date is necessary. This information would appear
approximately at tab (50) but because the headings vary in length,
it might be necessary to back the information off from the page
number leaving several spaces to separate the slug from the page
number.

Occasionally, the revision heading or slug will be so long that it
will extend across most of the page. Therefore, that information
must appear, by virtue of its length, at the left direction margin
tab (19).

116A - Page Heading - Minimum Information

Rev. 11/11/77   32.

116B - Page Heading - Full Information

"The Hunters" - Rev. 11/11/77   32.

LITTLE HOUSE - "The Hunters" - Rev. 11/11/77   32.

REVISION PAGES: ASTERISKS

How to Use Asterisks To Indicate Changes

Preliminary Information

Even though revision pages are color coded to indicate that changes have
occurred on those pages, asterisks are also used to designate the
specific material changed.   Either the customer will asterisk the
changed material if the original page has been retyped or the typist
will know that the material handwritten in is changed.   Unless the
revised material on a given page is fairly obvious, the typist will have
no way of knowing what has been changed, therefore, the customer will
have to asterisk the material.

Asterisks should fall in a straight vertical line down the right hand
side of the page at tab (78).

Asterisking Line Changes Only

Specific lines that have been changed are asterisked directly across
from the specific line changes.   (See Example 118A opposite)

The 2/3 Rule

(a)   Asterisk by the Character Cue When...

                ... a character's dialogue is changed completely in
                places or at least 2/3 changed. The asterisk should be
                placed on the same line as the character cue.   (See
                Example 118B opposite)

(b)   Asterisk by the Scene Number When...

                ... more than 2/3 of a scene is changed or when a scene
                has been omitted completely.   By the same token if a
                scene has been added creating an "A" scene, that scene
                must also incorporate an asterisk after the scene number
                since the material was not there before.   (See 118C
                opposite)

(c)   Asterisk by the Page Number When...

                ... more than 2/3 of a page is been changed.   The
                asterisk should fall after the page number at tab
                (78). Asterisking the page number eliminates a plethora
                of asterisks cascading down the side of the page.

118A - Asterisking A Line Change

47.

                    GULLIVER (O.S.)
                  (calling)
          These ropes are a little tight.   *

118B - 2/3 Or More Dialogue Change - Asterisk Character Cue

                        LILLIPUTIAN #1   *
          Your complaints are futile. The
          people are not allowed to voice
          complaints.

118C - 2/3 Or More Scene Change - Asterisk Scene Number

247   EXT. LILLIPUT - DAY   247 *

       A fire is raging nearby out of control. The bucket
       brigade works feverishly.

147A   CLOSE ANGLE - GULLIVER   247A *

                        GULLIVER
          I think I have the answer.

Asterisking Lines Or Paragraphs Omitted

When a line or lines have been deleted, and a natural spacing occurs immediately after, the asterisk should appear on the blank line to indicate that something is missing. (See Example 120A opposite)

Exceptions

There may be requests to use asterisks differently than the standard ways previously mentioned. Some production personnel use two or three asterisks on the same line which may indicated to them the number of times changes have been made. In these cases of departure, the asterisks should be handled according to the way they appear in the original script.

120A - Lines Or Paragraphs Deleted

248   EXT. LILLIPUT - MOMENTS LATER   248

All that remains of the fire are a few smoldering
ashes.

                                                                *

249   CLOSE ANGLE - GULLIVER   249

A sense of accomplishment if not relief can be seen in
his face.

<u>EXERCISE: REVISION PAGES</u>

The following five pages numbered 52 through 56 at the upper right
corner are revision pages as a typist might receive them. Type
these pages in correct format using scene numbers on both sides.
The revision slug to be used on each page is: "The Meeting" -
Rev. 3/11/80. Asterisks are to be used for changes... asterisk
only where asterisks appear. Add the new, written material and
delete the old. Tighten up the pages so that no large blank areas
occur until the end of the run.

37   INT. INN - NIGHT - ON KATE   37

as she moves to pour herself a healthy slug from the
bar set up on the piano. Mario is still very much
concerned with himself.

                    MARIO
          Boy, something like that really
          brings you up short.
                    (holds out shaking
                    hands)
          I mean look at me! I tell you,
          Kate, when she started talking about
          the good fairy... well, it affected
          me in a very profound way.

                    KATE
          Mario, I have three children too.

                    MARIO
          What do you want me to do, Kate?

                    KATE
          I think it might be a terrific idea
          if you stopped talking about it.
          It's only making you feel worse.

                    MARIO
          I can't feel any worse. That pure
          little voice saying...

He sees her expression, stops, tries to shake it off
with a jerk of his head.   ⊗ ←——————— KATE
                                  (concerned but firm)
                    MARIO   Mario!
                    (continuing)
          No, you're right. Forget it.
          Talk about something else. Tell
          me the good story about Harry.

During the following Mario tries to concentrate but is
still obviously nervous and distracted.

                    KATE
          Okay. He went bankrupt.

                    MARIO
          He went bankrupt? Harry went
          actually bankrupt?

Kate takes a long draw on her drink.

                    Ⓧ ←

                                        (CONTINUED)

[Handwritten insert, linked to ⊗ marks:]

MARIO
(continuing quizzically)
How can you go bankrupt
selling TV sets?
KATE
It's his heart. He has
a big heart. Talks people
out of buying things
they can't afford.
(reflectively)
It's one of the things
I like best about him.
MARIO
That's the good story?
KATE
That's it.

38/39 OMITTED

40   INT. AIRPORT TERMINAL - DAY   40

        Mario stands in line with Kate at the ticket counter.
        He glances about as if to somehow pull a solution to
        his problem out of the air.

                        MARIO
                I have a miserable case of
                indigestion.

                        KATE
                Cheer up, Mario... it's not the
                end of the world. I'm not leaving
                you permanently.
                        (a beat)
                I'll see you next year.

                        MARIO
                No, I don't think you will.

                        KATE
                Just because I have to leave early
                one year, you're willing to throw
                away a lifetime of weekends?
                        (beat)
                That kind of thinking would give
                anyone indigestion.

                        MARIO
                        (loudly)
                I don't have indigestion...
                        (quietly)
                ... anymore.

41   ANGLE - TICKET AGENT   41

        Trying to hassle the phones and breaking into the
        conversation between Mario and Kate long enough to at
        least find out where she is going and whether or not
        she prefers "smoking" or "non-smoking".

                        AGENT
                Yes... could I help... Ma'am...
                What is your destination?

                        KATE
                Destiny is more like it.

                        MARIO
                Cedar Rapids. One way to Cedar
                Rapids. Non-smoking.

                                        (CONTINUED)

                        -123-

41   CONTINUED: 41

                              AGENT
                    Right. Here you are, sir.

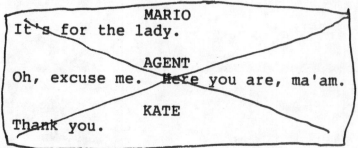

                              MARIO
                    It's for the lady.

                              AGENT
                    Oh, excuse me. ~~Here~~ you are, ma'am.

                              KATE
                    Thank you.

          They head for the gate.

42   ANGLE - MARIO AND KATE   42

                              MARIO
                    How can you be so casual?

                              KATE
                    I don't see any point in going on.
          Switch the suitcase from one hand to the other shaking his head.
          He moves to ~~get the suitcase shaking his head.~~

                              MARIO
                    Don't do that to me, Kate. Don't
                    try to manipulate me. I get
                    enough of that at home.

                              KATE
                    Mario, what's the point of meeting
                    in guilt and remorse? What joy is
                    there in that?

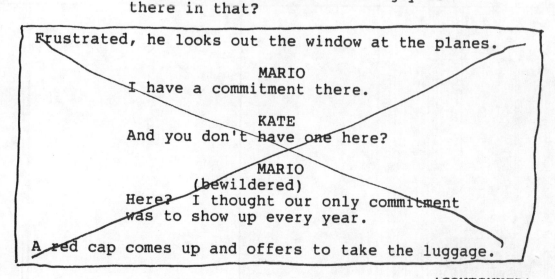

          Frustrated, he looks out the window at the planes.

                              MARIO
                    I have a commitment there.

                              KATE
                    And you don't have one here?

                              MARIO
                              (bewildered)
                    Here? I thought our only commitment
                    was to show up every year.

          A red cap comes up and offers to take the luggage.

                                                    (CONTINUED)

42   CONTINUED: MARIO   42
                          I don't know what to say.

Mario hands him the bags reaching into his pocket for a
tip. The red cap leaves. Kate and Mario continue
toward the gate.

                    KATE
          Nice and tidy, eh? An annual
          flight... no strings.

                    MARIO
          Okay, so maybe I was kidding
          myself. I'm human after all.

                    KATE
          Right, me, too. Or didn't you
          notice.

                    MARIO
          Well, of course, but you're
          different. Stronger. You... you
          always seem to sort of... well...
          cope better than I. I mean...
          there are just some things I...
          well, I seem to have trouble
          meeting head on.

                    KATE
          Which things don't you have
          trouble meeting head on? Give me
          a hint.

                    MARIO
          Oh, God, I feel so guilty.

He pauses momentarily and leans against the wall unable to cope.
indeed to meeting anything head on... at least for the
moment... or ever it seems.

                    KATE
          Sometimes I feel guilty too. All
          those times I wanted to pick up
          the phone and call you. But
          you're right, I do cope.
                    (intensely)
          You're trying to cope with the
          situation. What you should be
          doing is to let this all between
          us just "be". That's the beauty
          of it. That it can just "be". It
          seems to me that what you have to
          cope with is your guilt.

                              (CONTINUED)

43   INT. AIRPORT - GATE   43

Kate moves through the gate to board the plane. Mario
holds her back.

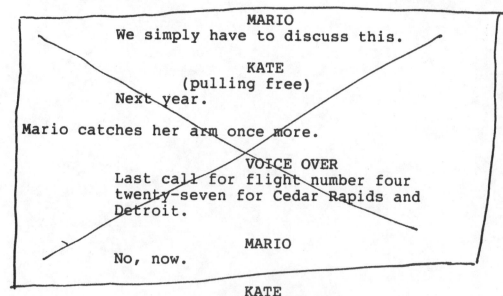

                          MARIO
          We simply have to discuss this.

                          KATE
                       (pulling free)
          Next year.

Mario catches her arm once more.

                          VOICE OVER
          Last call for flight number four
          twenty-seven for Cedar Rapids and
          Detroit.

                          MARIO
          No, now.

                          KATE
                    (pulling free again)
          I have to go. The plane is leaving!

Defeated, Mario lets go.

                          KATE
                       (continuing)
          Next year, I promise.

She runs back, kisses him tenderly and runs for the
plane.

44   OMITTED   44

45   EXT. AIRPORT TERMINAL - ON MARIO   45

searching for a cab among a sea of people who all have
the same idea. Finally he races across the street and
jumps into a cab whose passengers have barely had time
to get out.

                          CAB DRIVER
          Where to, buddy?

                          MARIO
          Cedar Rapids.

                          CAB DRIVER
          This thing don't fly, you know.

THE KEY TO THE PREVIOUS EXERCISE

IS ON THE FOLLOWING FIVE PAGES

37   INT. INN - NIGHT - ON KATE   37

as she moves to pour herself a healthy slug from the
bar set up on the piano. Mario is still very much
concerned with himself.

                    MARIO
          Boy, something like that really
          brings you up short.
                    (holds out shaking
                    hands)
          I mean look at me! I tell you,
          Kate, when she started talking about
          the good fairy... well, it affected
          me in a very profound way.

                    KATE
          Mario, I have three children too.

                    MARIO
          What do you want me to do, Kate?

                    KATE
          I think it might be a terrific
          idea if you stopped talking about
          it. It's only making you feel
          worse.

                    MARIO
          I can't feel any worse. That pure
          little voice saying...

He sees her expression, stops, tries to shake it off
with a jerk of his head.

                    KATE
                    (concerned but   *
                    firm)
          Mario!

                    MARIO
          No, you're right. Forget it.
          Talk about something else. Tell
          me the good story about Harry.

During the following Mario tries to concentrate but is
still obviously nervous and distracted.

                    KATE
          Okay. He went bankrupt.

                                        (CONTINUED)

37   CONTINUED: 37

                              MARIO
                    He went bankrupt? Harry went
                    actually bankrupt?

          Kate takes a long draw on her drink.

                              MARIO
                         (continuing;
                          quizzically)
                    How can you go bankrupt selling TV
                    sets?

                              KATE
                    It's his heart. He has a big
                    heart. Talks people out of buying
                    things they can't afford.
                         (reflectively)
                    It's one of the things I like best
                    about him.

                              MARIO
                    That's a good story?

                              KATE
                    That's it.

"The Meeting" - Rev. 3/11/80   53.

38   OMITTED   38   *
AND   AND
39   39

40   INT. AIRPORT TERMINAL - DAY   40

Mario stands in line with Kate at the ticket counter.
He glances about as if to somehow pull a solution to
his problem out of the air.

                        MARIO
              I have a miserable case of
              indigestion.

                        KATE
              Cheer up, Mario... it's not the
              end of the world. I'm not leaving
              you permanently.
                        (a beat)
              I'll see you next year.

                        MARIO
                        (quietly)
              No, I don't think you will.

                        KATE
              Just because I have to leave early
              one year, you're willing to throw
              away a lifetime of weekends?

                                                                    *

41   ANGLE - TICKET AGENT   41

Trying to hassle the phones and breaking into the
conversation between Mario and Kate long enough to at
least find out where she is going and whether or not
she prefers "smoking" or "non-smoking".

                        AGENT
              Yes... could I help... Ma'am...
              What is your destination?

                        KATE
              Destiny is more like it.

                        MARIO
              Cedar Rapids. One way to Cedar
              Rapids. Non-smoking.

                                            (CONTINUED)

"The Meeting" - Rev. 3/11/80   54.

41   CONTINUED: 41

                         AGENT
                  Right. Here you are, sir.

They head for the gate.   *

42   ANGLE - MARIO AND KATE   42

                         MARIO
                  How can you be so casual?

                         KATE
                  I don't see any point in going on.

He moves to switch the suitcase from one hand to the   *
other shaking his head.

                         MARIO
                  Don't do that to me, Kate. Don't
                  try to manipulate me. I get
                  enough of that at home.

                         KATE
                  Mario, what's the point of meeting
                  in guilt and remorse? What joy is
                  there in that?

                         MARIO   *
                  I don't know what to say.

                         KATE
                  Nice and tidy, eh? An annual
                  fling... no strings.

                         MARIO
                  Okay, so maybe I was kidding
                  myself. I'm human after all.

                         KATE
                  Right, me, too. Or didn't you
                  notice.

                         MARIO
                  Well, of course, but you're
                  different. Stronger. You... you
                  always seem to sort of... well...
                  cope better than I. Oh, God, I   *
                  feel so guilty.

                                        (CONTINUED)

                         -131-

42   CONTINUED: 42

He pauses momentarily and leans against the wall unable   *
to cope.

                         KATE
               Sometimes I feel guilty too. All
               those times I wanted to pick up
               the phone and call you. But
               you're right, I do cope.
                    (intensely)
               You're trying to cope with the
               situation. What you should be
               doing is to let this all just   *
               "be". That's the beauty of it.
               That it can just "be". It seems
               to me that what you have to cope
               with is your guilt.

43   INT. AIRPORT - GATE   43

Kate moves through the gate to board the plane. Mario
holds her back.

                         KATE   *
                    (pulling free)   *
               I have to go. The plane is leaving!

Defeated, Mario lets go.

                         KATE
                    (continuing)
               Next year, I promise.

She runs back, kisses him tenderly and runs for the
plane.

44   OMITTED   44   *

45   EXT. AIRPORT TERMINAL - ON MARIO   45

searching for a cab among a sea of people who all have
the same idea. Finally he races across the street and
jumps into a cab whose passengers have barely had time
to get out.

                         CAB DRIVER
               Where to, buddy?

                         MARIO
               Cedar Rapids.

                                                                 *

HOW TO CONSTRUCT
A SHOOTING SCHEDULE FROM
BREAKDOWN SHEETS

Preliminaries

Unless you find yourself typing for a professional script service, you probably won't be involved with typing a shooting schedule. A sample schedule is included in this section along with some general information just so that you may get a basic idea of how a schedule is worked out and finally set up in correct format. Should you ever need to type one, you will have the general idea of how to do it from the background informtion and the sample pages of schedule typed from breakdown sheets, all of which follow.

SHOOTING SCHEDULES

General Information

A shooting schedule is exactly what the name implies: A day by day schedule set up for the filming of a movie production. The director works out the shooting sequence on special forms known as breakdown sheets.

Location for the most part dictates the order of shooting since some scenes may be filmed in a particular locale or in an area of the country many miles away. Logically, then, those scenes will all be shot while the company is at that particular location. Because of this location consideration the scenes are not shot in the chronological sequence of the script.

Format - First Page

Tabs (11, 21, 41, 61)

The heading on the first page of a shooting schedule must contain the specific information requested by the production company. The date of the schedule (usually the date it is typed) should appear at (61). (See Example 136A opposite)

Other heading information involves the inclusive shooting dates and the listing of certain production personnel. (See Examples 136A and 136B opposite for placement and format.) Notice that a **solid** underscore separates this information from the body of the schedule.

The body of the schedule begins with "1ST DAY", the day of the week and the numeric indication of the month, day and year. Across from that (41) is the location. (See Examples opposite for placement and format.) Notice again that a solid underscore is placed under this information.

What follows on the next page is the heading information which would be sent along with the breakdown sheets. The heading information tells you what is required on the first page of the schedule. Beginning on page 142 are several pages of sample breakdown sheets.

```
┌─────────────────────────────────────────────────────────┐
│ 136A - 1st Page Heading - Feature Length movie │
└─────────────────────────────────────────────────────────┘
```

August 7, 1980

GERMANE PRODUCTIONS

"Murder In Micronesia"

SHOOTING SCHEDULE

PROD. #1756-08

```
SHOOTS:                        EXEC. PROD.:   H.M. Rose
TUESDAY, SEPT. 16, 1980        PRODUCER:      Ronald Higgins
THRU                           DIRECTOR:      Pamela Wise
WEDNESDAY, OCT. 9, 1980        ASS'T DIR.:    J.A. Wolfe
```
_____

1ST DAY, TUESDAY, 9/16/80   LOC: Simi Valley

_____


```
┌─────────────────────────────────────────────────────────┐
│ 136B - 1st Page Heading - Series Film Show │
└─────────────────────────────────────────────────────────┘
```

December 13, 1979

NBC-TV PRODUCTIONS

LITTLE HOUSE ON THE PRAIRIE

"The Pride Of Walnut Grove"

PROD. #7512

SHOOTING SCHEDULE

```
                               PRODUCER:      Miles McKray
SHOOTS:                        DIRECTOR:      Lyle Laundon
WEDNESDAY, FEB. 5, 1980        ASSOC. PROD.:  Van Tedlander
THRU
THURSDAY, FEB. 15, 1980
```
_____

1ST DAY - WEDNESDAY, 2/5/80   LOC: STG. 15

_____

Format - Body

Under the day of shooting, date and location slug appears the scenes and the people and other necessary bits of information necessary for the shooting of that scene.

For placement and format of the items listed below, refer to the sample shooting schedule "A Little Knight Music" following the breakdown sheets on pages 151 through 153.

Notice that the information is basically a single spaced format with double spacing between the different elements of categories. The first item is a master scene slug (no camera angles please), time of day, and the number of pages that particular scene or scenes cover, broken down into eighths of a page. The next listing is the scene number or numbers and a short synopsis of the scene or scenes.

Now appear the headings or categories of information, any or all of which may be used according to the requirements of the scene.

CAST -- a listing of the characters who appear in the scene. Numbers are assigned to each character and these numbers should appear in chronological order. CAST is always the first category and no other category may be listed under it.

BITS -- people with bit parts or doubles for characters. These are usually non-speaking parts.

ATMOS. -- (ATMOSPHERE) which involves the background characters (extras) used to fill out the scene.

PROPS -- certain specific objects which may include breakaways... chairs, vases, etc.

If there is no ATMOS. or PROPS, others of the following categories may move up into that area.

LIVESTOCK -- if animals, wagons, carriages, buckboards, etc., are being used.

VEHICLES -- automobiles, trucks and the like.

SPFX. -- special effects such as smoke, thunder, etc.

Again notice that a solid underscore separates the master scenes being shot.

Miscellaneous items

NOTE: Should there be a note to the director or technicians, it appears double spaced under the scene synopsis.
(See sample for format and placement)

TRAVEL DAY -- occasionally travel days are noted on the
schedule to indicate that the company will be moving from
one location to another. Hopefully it works out that
only a quarter of a page is used. If not, a whole page
will have to be used to indicate a travel day. The same
holds true when a holiday falls in the shooting schedule.

Notice Also That:

1) The shooting schedule is numbered consecutively.

2) On subsequent pages of a shooting day, the heading of
the pages restate the title of the film and production number if there is one, and the shooting day
(1ST DAY, 2ND DAY, etc.) are slugged at the top along
with the word (CONT'D).

3) Whenever the location of the shooting changes, it must
be stated. (See Example page 152)

4) The end of a given shooting day along with the total
number of script pages (in eighths) is slugged between
solid underscore lines.

5) A new day always begins a new page.

6) If a television series shooting more than one episode,
the episode number and/or title must be clearly stated
so that the production staff knows which scenes are
from what episode.

SHOOTING SCHEDULES

Heading Information: "A Little Knight Music"

                                            July 30, 1980

                  FUTURE KING PRODUCTIONS

                  "A Little Knight Music"

                      Prod. #428-81

                  SHOOTING SCHEDULE

SHOOTS: PRODUCER: Michael Markovitch
MONDAY, AUG. 7, 1981   DIRECTOR: Collin Hill
THRU   ASST. DIR: W.J. Finch
THURSDAY, SEPT. 2, 1981   PROD. MGR: Roland Williams

Attached to the breakdown sheets for each day's shooting is a slip of paper (below) with the day of shooting, the date, and the total number of script pages covered that day. (See the shooting schedule example pages 151 and 152 for placement of this information)

```
1ST DAY


    MONDAY 8/7/81


TOTAL PAGES:  8 7/8
```

SHOOTING SCHEDULE

Breakdown Sheets - Explanation

Breakdown sheets are special forms the director uses to set up the schedule. It is from these initial formidable looking sheets that the shooting schedule information is taken. The page numbers on the breakdown sheets are not usually in chronological sequence, so great care must be taken not to get them out of order!

Each day's shooting will be clipped together with a scrap of paper indicating the day of shooting, the day of the week, and the numeric indication of the date with the total number of script pages covered.

The heading information also will be recorded on a separate sheet of paper since the breakdown sheets have no space to accommodate it.

Production Title	Page No.
"A Little Knight Music"	

Set	Total Sequences	Location
Ext. Tournament – D		Simi Valley

Period	Season	
		3 1/8 Pgs.

#1 Arthur
 2 Guinevere
 3 Lancelot
 4 Sir Eetor
 5 Sir Kay
 6 Sir Gwaine
 7 Sir Bedevere
 8 Merlin
 9 Archbishop of
    Cantebury

Atmos
15 Knights
 8 Heralds
10 Esquires at
    Arms
___
33 Total

Bits
DBL: Lancelot

Livestock
27 Horses

2 Members
  Aspca

Special Props
27 Banners
12 Pennants
 8 15th Century
    Military
    Trumpets

Note: Use fish eye lens in scene #109

Sequences – Scenes – Synopses

#107 – 110 Lancelot proves his expertise
            with a sword and wins
            approval from Guinevere.

Production Title			Page No.
Set EXT. CATHEDRAL ~ D.	Total Sequences Location Simi Valley		
Period Season	5 ⁵⁄₈ Pgs.		

<u>Cast</u>

#1 Arthur

8 Merlin

9 Archbishop of Cantebury

12 Sir Elfius

<u>Atmos</u>

27 townspeople

Special Props

Sword

Stone

Sequences - Scenes - Synopses

Sens. # 22 - 25 - Arthur pulls the sword from the "marble stone" proving himself the "heir apparent" of Uther-Pendragon

Production Title			Page No.
Set EXT. COUNTRYSIDE – D.		Total Sequences Location	
Period	Season		1/8 Pg.

Cast
#1 Arthur

BITS

3 Young Boys

LIVESTOCK

4 horses

Special Props

Sequences – Scenes – Synopses

Sc. #1 – Young Arthur & his companions ride
like the wind through the countryside

Production Title			Page No.
Set		Total Sequences Location	
Period	Season		

			Special Props

Company travels to Los Angeles

Sequences - Scenes - Synopses

```
2ND DAY

    TUESDAY 8/8/81

TOTAL PAGES:  4
```

Production Title			Page No.

Set EXT. CAMELOT LAGOON - D.   **Total Sequences Location** LOC: Toluca Lake / Lake

Period   **Season**

1½ Pgs.

<u>CAST</u> #1 Arthur 2 Guinevere			
		<u>Livestock</u> Horse & Carriage	**Special Props** Picnic Basket Food Stuffs Book of Poetry

Sequences - Scenes - Synopses

Se. #92 - Arthur & Guinevere picnicking by the lagoon talking of life & love. All's well in Camelot.

Production Title			Page No.
Set		Total Sequences Location	
EXT. CASTLE OF CAMELIARD –			
Period	Season		2 6/8 Pgs.

CAST

#2 Guinevere

10 King Leodegrance

14 Duke of North
    Umber

Atmos

23 townspeople

Bits

6 Knights.
Companion

Livestock

6 horses

Special Props

Sequences – Scenes – Synopses

Scns 53 & 54 – The Duke of North Umber & and
his 6 "Knights-Companion" arrive
on the field to do battle. King
Leodegrance is in trouble!
Guinevere consoles him.

Set   Total Sequences Location

EXT. CAMELOT LAGOON - D.

Period   Season

½ Pg.

| | | Livestock | |
| | | Horse & Carriage | Special Props |

Sequences - Scenes - Synopses

Sc. #91   Camelot Lagoon - Establishing

ON THE NEXT PAGE IS THE SHOOTING SCHEDULE

FOR "A LITTLE KNIGHT MUSIC" TYPED IN CORRECT

FORMAT. ALL INFORMATION IS CORRECTLY PLACED.

COMPARE IT WITH THE INFORMATION ON THE BREAK-

DOWN SHEETS.

July 30, 1980

FUTURE KING PRODUCTIONS

"A Little Knight Music"

Prod. #428-81

SHOOTING SCHEDULE

SHOOTS: PRODUCER: Michael Markovitch
MONDAY, AUG. 7, 1981   DIRECTOR: Collin Hill
THRU   ASST. DIR: W.J. Finch
THURSDAY, SEPT. 2, 1981   PROD. MGR: Roland Williams

1ST DAY - MONDAY, 8/7/81   LOC: SIMI VALLEY

EXT. TOURNAMENT - DAY - 3 1/8 PGS.

Scs. #107 thru #110 - Lancelot proves his expertise
with a sword and wins approval from Guinevere.

NOTE: USE FISH EYE LENS IN SC. #109

CAST   BITS   SPFX:
#1 ARTHUR   DBL: Lancelot   Wind furling
#2 GUINEVERE   banners
#3 LANCELOT   ATMOS.
#4 SIR ECTOR   15 Knights   2 Members ASPCA
#5 SIR KAY   8 Heralds
#6 SIR GWAINE   10 Esquires at   PROPS
#7 SIR BEDEVERE   Arms   27 Banners
#8 MERLIN   33 TOTAL   12 Pennants
#9 ARCHBISHOP OF   8 15th Century
   CANTEBURY   Military
                                              Trumpets

                                            LIVESTOCK
                                            27 Horses

EXT. CATHEDRAL - DAY - 5 5/8 PGS.

Scs. #22 thru #25 - Arthur pulls the sword from the
marble stone proving himself the heir apparent of
Uther-Pendragon.

CAST   ATMOS.   PROPS
#1 ARTHUR   27 townspeople   Sword
#8 MERLIN   Stone
#9 ARCHBISHOP OF
    CANTEBURY
#10 SIR ELFIUS

EXT. COUNTRYSIDE - DAY - 1/8 PG.

Sc. #1 - Young Arthur and his companions ride like
the wind through the countryside.

CAST	BITS	LIVESTOCK
#1 ARTHUR	3 Young boys	4 Horses

END OF 1ST DAY   TOTAL PAGES: 8 7/8

COMPANY TRAVELS TO LOS ANGELES

EXT. CAMELOT - DAY - 1 1/8 PGS.

Sc. #92 - Arthur and Guinevere picnicking by the
lagoon talking of life and love. All's well in
Camelot.

CAST	PROPS	LIVESTOCK
#1 ARTHUR	Picnic basket	Horse/carriage
#2 GUINEVERE	Food stuffs	
	Book of poetry	

EXT. CASTLE OF CAMELIARD - DAY - 2 6/8 PGS.

Scs. #53 & #54 - The Duke of North Umber and his six
"Knights-Companion" arrive on the field to do battle.
King Leodegrance is in trouble! Guinevere consoles
him.

CAST	BITS	LIVESTOCK
#2 GUINEVERE	6 Knights-Companion	6 Horses
#10 KING		
LEODEGRANCE	ATMOS.	
#14 DUKE OF	23 townspeople	
NORTH UMBER		

EXT. CAMELOT LAGOON - DAY - 1/8 PG.

Sc. #91 - Establishing shot of Camelot Lagoon.

LIVESTOCK
Horse/Carriage

END OF 2ND DAY   TOTAL PAGES: 4

THE COMPLETE GUIDE TO STANDARD SCRIPT FORMATS

PART II

TAPED FORMATS FOR TELEVISION

This volume explains in detail how to set up video taped formats
for television. These two basic formats are used for sitcoms,
variety, award and special shows. There are examples also of
special pages required when the script goes into production.
These pages include short rundowns,
rehearsal and taping schedules, staff and crew lists.

Foreword by Viki King, author of

HOW TO WRITE A MOVIE IN 21 DAYS
and
BEYOND VISUALIZATION

To order any of these books see next page.

ORDER FORM

To order **THE COMPLETE GUIDE TO STANDARD SCRIPT FORMATS -
PART I (Screenplays) _or_ PART II (Taped formats for TV)** send check or
money order to:

CMC Publishing   PRICE: $18.95
11642 Otsego Street   Plus $2.00 shipping/handling
N. Hollywood, CA 91601   (CA residents add sales tax)

Name _____Address_____

City, State, Zip_____

_____ Part I (Screenplays)   _____Part II (Taped formats for TV)

ORDER FORM

BOOKS BY VIKI KING
_____   **HOW TO WRITE A MOVIE IN 21 DAYS**   **$10.95**
_____   **BEYOND VISUALIZATION**   **$10.95**

   Add: $2.00 per book shipping/handling

AUDIO CASSETTES
_____   **THE 9-MINUTE MOVIE**   **$9.95**
                What Goes on Pages 1,3,10,30,45,60,75,90,120

_____   **NO MORE WRITER'S BLOCK**   **$9.95**
                How to Embrace the Impossible Obstacles

_____   **WHAT'S THE STORY**   **$9.95**
                How to Know What You Want to Say and Say It

   Add: $1.50 per tape shipping/handling

SPECIAL PACKAGE: Order all 3 tapes plus one of the books for $39.95 plus $5.00
                shipping/handling. Indicate which book you want.

   California residents add sales tax

Send check or money order to: Viki King
                                  P.O. Box 563
                                  Malibu, California 90265

Name _____Address_____

City, State, Zip_____

"A" PAGE — A term used to describe additional pages added to a script. The page number is used along with "A", "B", "C", and so on in order to keep the pages consecutive. Insures they will fit consecutively in previously distributed scripts.

AD LIB — Extemporaneous lines or phrases appropriate to a given situation. There may, for example, be AD LIB greetings when guests arrive at a party.

b.g. background — Any activity or sound in a scene that is secondary or subordinate to the main action and which serves as a backdrop for that action. Used in direction, always abbreviated in lower case followed by periods after each letter.

CLOSE SHOT — A camera shot involving just the shoulders and head of a character. Similar but not to be confused with CLOSEUP. Always spelled out and capitalized.

CLOSEUP — A camera shot that closely examines and/or emphasizes some detail either on a person or an inanimate object. Incorrectly used abbreviated but correctly spelled out and capitalized.

COMBINATION PAGE — A page which is assigned two or more consecutive page numbers to account for pages that have been deleted from the script as a result of editing. May be stated pages: 11/12., or 85-87.

CONDENSING — "Cheating" on spacing to make a screenplay type out to fewer pages. Does not reflect an accurate page count.

DISSOLVE: — A scene ending used to indicate that the scene should gradually fade away.

DOLLY (DOLLIES)	A camera cue used in direction instructing the camera to move along with the subject or subjects of the scene. This is achieved by using either a handheld camera or a camera secured to an apparatus on wheels. Always capitalized in direction.
ELLIPSIS	A series of three periods used to signify a pause or change in thought sequence. Use of the ellipsis often indicates that a word or words have been left out because they are "understood".
EXT. (EXTERIOR)	Indicates that a particular scene takes place outdoors. Used in scene headings, always abbreviated, followed by a period and capitalized.
EXTREME CLOSEUP	The camera is in very close, usually on an object, for purposes of spotlighting a detail. Incorrectly stated: E.C.U. or ECU, but correctly spelled out and capitalized.
EXTREME LONG SHOT	Camera angle that involves shooting an "all encompassing" scene from considerable distance away. Sometimes incorrectly: XLS or ELS but correctly must appear spelled out and capitalized.
FADE OUT.	A scene ending used at the end of an act and at the end of a film. Should not really appear in the middle of a script (without acts) since FADE TO: is more correctly used. FADE OUT. means that the scene gradually darkens to black. Always spelled out, capitalized, followed by a period.
FILM FORMAT	The specific script format used for a one camera production. A term used interchangeably with screenplay, one camera, and feature film format.
f.g. (foreground)	Those activities which take place nearest the viewer in perspective. Focus here may also be an object. Opposite of background. Used in direction. Always abbreviated, followed by periods, lower case.

FREEZE FRAME.   Works as a camera direction rather than a scene ending. It means that the picture stops moving and becomes a still photograph in effect, holding for a given period of time.

HOLD   To keep the same. Applies to scene and page numbers in revisions. To "hold" the scene numbers means to keep them the same as they appear in the script. The reason to hold scene numbers is that the script has already been broken down into shooting sequence (boarded) and to change the scene numbers on the script would necessitate the task of changing them on the boards.

INSERT   A scene involving an inanimate object which gives us a certain piece of information or calls our attention to a specific fact. The insert may be a watch telling the time, a calendar, a diamond ring, etc.

INT.   Indicates that a particular scene will be shot
(INTERIOR)   indoors. Used in scene headings, always abbreviated, capitalized and followed by a period.

LONG SHOT   A camera angle shot from some distance usually including considerable background detail. Capitalized and spelled out.

MASTER SCENE   Usually "major" scenes which designate a location where several shots/angles may take place. Begins with INT. or EXT.

MATCH CUT: Involves matching the subject of one scene to the subject of the next scene. For example, we may see a unique brooch being worn at a dinner party in one scene, then cut to the next scene where we see the same brooch in a pawn shop window.

MED. SHOT   A shot of one or two characters from the waist up. The only camera angle that is abbreviated. Always capitalized and abbreviated.

MONTAGE

Two or more related subjects on the screen at the same time blended in a montage effect. MONTAGE is a scene heading. The end of the montage must be indicated in capital letters isolated at the direction margin. (END OF MONTAGE is not be numbered as a scene.)

M.O.S.

Essentially without sound. Indistinguishable dialogue may be heard. In the early days of film making derived from German directors who wanted a scene shot "mit out sound".

MOVING
MOVING SHOT

A camera cue used in direction to dictate that the camera should move with the subject being filmed.

O.C.
(OFF CAMERA)

Sounds or dialogue heard while the camera is on another subject. Same as off screen, however, off camera is the term used in three camera television formats. Capitalized, abbreviated, followed by periods.

O.S.
(OFF SCREEN)

Same as off camera. Correct term used in screenplays and one camera film formats. A character talks from an adjacent area while the camera is on someone or something else. Sounds may be O.S. too. Stated: (O.S.) next to the character cue and O.S. in direction. Capitalized, abbreviated and followed by periods.

PAN

The camera moves slowly from left to right or vice versa, not stopping on any one thing or person. (Panorama.) Always capitalized and spelled out.

POV
(POINT OF VIEW)

The viewpoint of a character or characters. We, the audience, see something through this character's eyes, as he sees it. Always capitalized and abbreviated.

REVERSE POV

A point of view shot turned 180° to show the original subject.

REVISION PAGES   Pages on which changes have been made. Revision
                        pages occur as the film is in production. Typed
                        page for page utilizing short pages or additional
                        "A" pages so that the pages will fit into
                        existing scripts. Color coded to keep track of
                        the changes and slugged at the top of the page
                        with Rev. and the date.

RUN   Several pages in consecutive sequence. Used with
                        reference to revision pages.

SERIES OF SHOTS   A series of short action sequences which serve to
                        move the audience quickly through time,
                        experience, stream of consciousness, etc.

SIMULTANEOUS   Two characters speaking at the same time.
DIALOGUE   Dialogue may be placed side by side on the script
                        page. Tabs must be set to accommodate this
                        situation.

SITCOM   A shortened term meaning situation comedy. Used
                        in television.

SHOOTING SCHEDULE   A day by day schedule of filming set up for a
                        film production.

SFX: Abbreviation for sound effects. Used in tape
(SOUND EFFECTS)   formats for television. Requires technical
                        reproduction of a sound usually dubbed onto the
                        sound track. Wind blowing, dishes crashing,
                        laser guns shooting are all sound effects.
                        Abbreviated and followed by a period.

SPFX: Abbreviation for special effects. Used in tape
(SPECIAL EFFECTS)   formats for television. Requires technical
                        reproduction of some kind. Smoke billowing from
                        under a door is a special effect. Abbreviated
                        and followed by a colon.

SPLIT SCREEN   One or more subjects shown on the screen
                        simultaneously with the screen divided into
                        separate actions. Split screen may utilize many
                        different subjects in many splits or the same
                        subject in many splits. "The Thomas Crown
                        Affair" employs split screen.

GLOSSARY

SUBJECTIVE CAMERA   The subjective camera becomes the eyes of a person, animal, or "scary thing" (most frequently the foe) which has not yet been introduced on camera. This technique is used to create suspense and a heightened sense of drama.

SUPER
(SUPERIMPOSE)   The effect is one of showing one thing over another in the same shot. More often than not the titles are "supered" over the beginning sequences of a film. Double spaced down, isolated at the direction margin, tab (19) and capitalized.

THREE CAMERA   One of the two specific script formats used for a taped television production. This term is used interchangeably with tape show or television format.

VOICE OVER
(V.O.)   Indicates a mechanical transmission of a voice heard over an instrument such as a telephone or tape recorder. Capitalized and spelled out in direction. Capitalized and abbreviated in parentheses next to the character name.

THE FOLLOWING APPENDICES
CAPSULIZE BASIC INFORMATION
PREVIOUSLY DISCUSSED

TAB SETTINGS

SCREENPLAYS

Tabs:

13	19	29	36	43	62	72	74
Scene Number	Direction	Dialogue	Personal direction	Character name	Scene endings/(CONTINUED)	Page number	Scene number

Cutoffs:

    (73)   (55)   (60)

SHOOTING SCHEDULES

8   21   41   61   73

TAPE FORMAT - STANDARD
(sometimes known as tape live)

11   16   31   73

TAPE FORMAT - VARIATION
(sometimes known as three camera)

11   21   36   61   73

UNIVERSAL TRUTHS

The following is a compendium of rules that consistently apply throughout all script formats. Most correspond with grammatical rules and some with script format rules. They are, in the long run, devised to promote clarity and consistency in script formats.

GENERAL

1) Do not break a sentence from one page to another. The sentence must be completed before going to the next page.

2) Always leave two spaces after the punctuation at the end of a sentence.

3) When using the ellipsis (three periods) to indicate a pause within a sentence or an understood word or thought, a space must be left after the last dot.

4) Dashes or hyphens may be also used to indicate a pause in the same way in which the ellipsis is used. Two dashes are used with a space on each side.

5) The word "okay" is always spelled out.

DIALOGUE (When in doubt, spell it out)

1) Spell out all one and two digit numbers. Three or more digits may be written numerically.

2) Spell out indications of time. Example: one-thirty.

3) Spell out all personal titles except: Mr., Mrs., and Ms.

4) Never hyphenate a word from one line to the next unless the word is normally hyphenated anyway. Example: son-in-law.

DIRECTION

1) Personal titles may be abbreviated. (Sgt., Capt.)

2) Words may be hyphenated from one line to the next but unless the word is unusually long, hyphenation isn't usually necessary for the most part.

CONDENSING

Condensing is a method sometimes used to "cheat" the length of a screenplay shorter. It is a practice that is frowned upon since it involves some distortion of format which consequently violates the one page = one minute of screen time formula. We mention condensing since it is a reality and should not be ignored. If condensing is requested of the typist by a client, the following methods are possible ways of doing it. (Presumably, the writer or whomever will have to reckon with that situation later!)

1)   Double space (instead of triple) between scenes.

2)   Make full pages.

3)   If scene numbers are not used, eliminate scene CONTINUEDS at the bottoms and tops of pages. (They aren't necessary in the absence of scene numbers anyway.)

4)   Eliminate the use of continuing for dialogue interrupted by direction.

(CONTINUED), CONTINUED:, (CONT'D), (continuing)

(CONTINUED) -- used only with reference to scenes. A scene is (CONTINUED) on tab (62) at the bottom of a page.

CONTINUED: -- used only with reference to scenes. Stated at the top of the page as CONTINUED: at margin (19) on line 6.

(CONT'D) -- used with reference to the breaking of dialogue from one page to the next. Always used with (MORE) + (CONTINUED) + (CONT'D)

EXAMPLE

                    Dialogue dialogue dialogue.
                         (MORE)

                                        (CONTINUED)

_____

        CONTINUED:

                              CHARACTER (CONT'D)

(continuing) -- appears in lower case and parenthesis at tab 36 under the character name anytime dialogue is interrupted by stage direction whether in the middle of the page or at the end of a page.

EXAMPLE

                        CHARACTER
              Dialogue dialogue dialogue

      Stage direction stage direction stage direction.

                        CHARACTER
                       (continuing)
              Dialogue dialogue dialogue.

OR:

                        CHARACTER
                    (continuing; beat)
              Dialogue dialogue dialogue.

ABBREVIATION, CAPITALIZATION AND PUNCTUATION

SCENE HEADINGS

Abbreviations

1) INT.
2) EXT.
3) MED. SHOT
4) POV
5) Personal titles

Capitalization

All words

Punctuation

1) dashes used to separate elements
2) parentheses used around:
   a) time of day, season, year
   b) (STOCK)

STAGE DIRECTION

Abbreviation

1) personal title
2) other standard abbreviations
3) b.g. - background
4) f.g. - foreground
5) O.S. - off screen

Spell out

1) sound cues
2) camera cues
3) character introductions
4) titles of songs, books, and movies
5) AD LIB
6) VOICE OVER

Punctuation

1) normal punctuation throughout
2) quotes around book, song and movie titles

CHARACTER CUE

Abbreviations

1) personal titles
2) (V.O.)
3) (O.S.)

Capitalization

All words

Punctuation

1) parenthesis around:
   a) (V.O.)
   b) (O.S.)
   c) specific role designation after character name

PERSONAL DIRECTION

Abbreviations

Personal titles

Capitalization

None except those that normally begin with a capital letter

Punctuation

Semicolon between continuing or beat and additional direction

DIALOGUE

Abbreviations; only

1) Mr.
2) Mrs.
3) Ms.

Spell out

All other words including:
1) two digit numbers
2) Personal titles
3) time indications
4) okay

<u>DIALOGUE</u> (CONT'D)

Capitalization

1) song, book, and movie titles
2) words used for emphasis

Punctuation

Normal punctuation or as per author

1) a space left after the ellipsis (three periods)
2) a space on each side of two dashes used to indicate a
   pause

SCENE ENDINGS

Abbreviations

None

Capitalization

ALL

Punctuation

Colon after all except FADE OUT. which is followed by a
period.

- A -

"A" PAGE
  defined 154
  explained in revisions 113
  example 129
ABBREVIATIONS
  (CONT'D) dialogue 91
  in character cues 75
  in stage direction:
    f.g., b.g., o.s., M.O.S., elsewhere 65
  of personal titles 162
  scene headings, words always
    abbreviated 27g
  Summary 166
ACT ONE - Screenplay
  use of 21
  tabs 21
AD LIB
  capitalize in direction 61
  definition 154
AERIAL SHOT
  definition 154
ANGLE/SHOT
  example 38L
ASTERISKS ON REVISIONS
2/3 Rule
  character cue 117
  exceptions 119
  for omitted items 119
  page number 117
  scene number 117
  tabs 117
ATMOS
  shooting schedules 137
  example 151
AUTHOR'S NAME
  not on screenplay cover 13
  on series cover 17
  on fly/title page

- B -

BACK TO SCENE
  explained 37H
  example 32
BITS
  defined 137
  example 151
b.g.
  definition 154
  example in direction 66
BREAKDOWN SHEETS
  explained 141
  examples 142-149
BREAKING DIALOGUE
  from one page to another 91, 164
  with stage direction 93
BUSINESS
  defined 53

- C -

CAMERA ANGLE
  in scene headings 29

CAMERA CUES
  capitalizing of in direction 57
  defined 7
  how to avoid missing 57
CAMERA
  is POV of audience 26
  must move after INSERTS and POV's 31
  subject of in scene headings 29
CAPITALIZATION
  AD LIB 61
  camera cues in direction 57
  character cues 77
  characters in direction 59
  CONTINUED: 47
  (CONTINUED) 47
  enters and exits 63
  FREEZE FRAME. 61
  in personal direction 81
  (MORE) 91
  NOTE to director 63
  scene headings 26A
  examples 28
  sound cues in direction 55
  sounds made by characters 55
  Summary 166
  TITLES 61
  (V.O.) and (O.S.) in character cue 75
CAST
  shooting schedules 137
  example 151
CHARACTER CUES
  definition 75
  format and tabs 75
  roles of character 77
  spelling and grammatical rules 167
CHARACTER INTRODUCTIONS
  capitalization of in direction 59
CHARACTERS
  when not to capitalize
    in direction 59
(CONT'D) DIALOGUE
  placement 91
CLOSE SHOT
  definition 154
  explained 38j
CLOSEUP
  definition 154
COLON
  after NOTE in stage direction 63
  after scene endings (transitions) 51
  with CONTINUED 47
COMBINATION PAGE
  definition 154
  example 132
  explained 113
CONDENSING/PACKING
  explained 154
  how to 163
CONTINUED: SCENES
  not used if no scene numbers 47
  on three or more pages 49
  use with scene numbers 47

(CONTINUED) SCENES
  format and tabs   47
  with (MORE)   91
  use of when stage direction breaks
    from one page to another   67
(CONTINUED), CONTINUED:,
(CONT'D) (continuing)
  Summary   164, 165
(continuing) DIALOGUE
  use of in dialogue breaks   93
  when not necessary   95
COVERS
  filmed series   17
  screenplay   13
CUT TO:
  use of   51

- D -

DASHES
  in dialogue as a pause   89f
  to break sentences in direction   67
DATE
  on fly/title page   19
  on revisions   115
  in scene headings   33
  on shooting schedules   135
  example   151
DIALOGUE
  breaking sentences in   89C
  definition   7, 87
  format and tabs   87
  indicating pauses in   89d/f
  interruption of with personal direction   89e
  spelling & grammatical rules   89, 166
DIRECTOR
  notes to   63
DISSOLVE TO:
  definition   154
DOLLY
  definition   155
DRAFT DATES AND NOTATION
  filmed series (cover)   17, 18
  title/fly page   19, 20

- E -

ELLIPSIS
  breaking sentences in direction   67
  definition   155
  in dialogue   89d/e
ENTERS/EXITS
  no capitalization   63
EPISODE TITLE
  shooting schedules   135
  series cover   17
ESTABLISHING SHOT
  explained   38
  ending a page with   26c
EXERCISES & KEYS
  revisions   121-132
  scene headings   43-46
  screenplay   102-110
  stage direction   71-73
EXT. (EXTERIOR)
  definition   155
  examples   36-38, 169

EXTREME CLOSEUP
  definition   155
  explained   38m
EXTREME LONG SHOT
  definition   155

- F -

FADE IN:, FADE OUT., FREEZE FRAME
  explanation & rules   51
FADE IN: - Screenplay
  page 1 - feature film   21
  television film in acts   21
FADE OUT.
  as scene ending   51
  definition   155
  ending acts   21
FADE TO: VS. FADE OUT.   51
f.g. (foreground)
  definition   155
  use in direction   65
FILM FORMAT
  comparison chart   9
  definition   6, 155
FIRST PAGE
  act one of filmed series   23
  act two of filmed series   23
  screenplay, no acts   21
  screenplay, with acts   21
  shooting schedule   135
FLASHBACKS   67, 68
FLY/TITLE PAGE
  example   20
  layout   19
FREEZE FRAME
  captalized in direction   61
  defined   156
  explained   51

- G -

GLOSSARY   154-159

- H -

HEADINGS
  revised pages   115
"HOLD" (PAGE & SCENE NUMBERS)
  definition   156
  explained   113
HYPHEN
  between page numbers on revisions   113
  in dialogue   89
  one line to next   162

- I -

INT. (INTERIOR)
  definition   156
  examples   36-38, 169
INT./EXT.
  explained in scene headings   37f
INT. OR EXT.
  in scene headings   26, 29
INSERT
  definition   156
  examples   39q
  scene headings following   31
  to end a page   26c

INTERCUT
  definition 40
  example 40
  in direction 40, 109
  in scene heading 40, 169

- L -

LONG SHOT
  definition 156
LIVESTOCK
  in shooting schedules 137
  example 151

- M -

MASTER SCENE 26
MATCH CUT
  definition 156
MED. SHOT (MEDIUM SHOT)
  definition 156
  example 38n
MONTAGE
  definition 157
  example 42
(MORE)
  when breaking dialogue 91
  tabs for 91
M.O.S. 91
MOVING OR MOVING SHOT
  definition 157

- N -

NOTE:
  in shooting schedules 138
  example 151
  to director (in direction) 63

- O -

O.C. (OFF CAMERA)
  definition 157
O.S. (OFF SCREEN OR OFF STAGE)
  definition 7, 157

- P -

PAGE 1 (SEE "FIRST PAGE")
PAGE NUMBERS
  filmed script 23
  of revisions 113
  omitted in revisions 113
PAN
  definition 157
PARAGRAPHING
  dialogue 89
  stage direction 57
PARENTHESES
  (continuing) in dialogue 93
  examples in scene headings 36c, 37d/e
  in character cues 77
  in notes to director 63
  in personal direction and (beat) 81, 95
  in scene headings 33
  Summary 166-167
  used with numbers after 49
  CONTINUED 49
  (V.O.) and (O.S.) in character cues 75

  with (CONT'D) in dialogue ?
  with (MORE) 9
PERIOD
  after FADE OUT. 51
  Summary 166-168
  with (V.O.) and (O.S.)
  in character cues 75
PERSONAL DIRECTION
  definition 7, 81
  do not end page with 85
  format and tabs 81
  "pulling out" long passages 83
POINT OF VIEW - POV
  example in scene headings 37g
  in scene headings 26
  scenes followinig POV shots 31
PRODUCTION COMPANY NAME
AND ADDRESS
  in shooting schedules 135
  not on cover 13
  on fly/title page 19
PRODUCTION NUMBER
  in shooting schedules 135
  on cover of series show
PROPS
  example 151
  in shooting schedule 137
PUNCTUATION
  Summary 166-168
  (See individual items, i.e. colon,
  period, etc.)

- R -

REVERSE POV 157
REVISION PAGES
  color code 112
  definitiion 158
"RUNS"
  definition 158
  explained 113

- S -

SCENE ENDINGS
  format and tabs 51
  ways to end scenes 51
SCENE HEADINGS
  abbreviations 27g
  at end of page 26c
  breaking 27f
  definition 26
  examples 36-41, 169
  format rules 26, 27
  margin and tabs 26d/e
  order 169
  parentheses 33
  segment order 33
  slashes 27j
  two entry example 36e
  two entry only 29
SCENE NUMBERS BOTH SIDES
  margin for direction 53
SCENE NUMBERS
  first scene number, tabs 21
  in revisions 113
  necessary 10, 31

SCENE NUMBERS (CONT'D)
  no period   27h
  one side or both?   10
SCENES
  added or omitted in revisions   113
SCREENPLAY - STANDARD FORMAT   102-106
SCREENPLAY - READING FORMAT   107-110
SECOND PAGE
  all acts or no acts   23
SENTENCES
  breaks in   67
SERIES OF SHOTS
  compared to MONTAGE   41
  definition   158
  examples   40/40s
SFX: (SOUND EFFECTS)   158
SHOOTING SCHEDULE   140
  breakdown sheets   142-149
  definition   135
  example, headings
    feature films   136a, 139
  example, heading
    filmed TV series   136B
  first page, format and tabs   135
  example correct typed format from
    breakdown sheets   151-153
  format notes   135-138
SHOT HEADING
  definition   26
SEMICOLON
  in personal direction   95
SIMULTANEOUS DIALOGUE
  definition   158
SITCOM
  definition   158
SLASHES
  in scene headings   27j
  on revisions   113
SLUGS (SCENE HEADINGS)
  definition   26
SOUND CUES
  capitalized in direction   55
  definition   7
SPACING
  after ellipsis   162
  between scenes - triple   26B
  between sentences   162
  in direction   53
SPELLING RULES   166-168
SPFX: (SPECIAL EFFECTS)
  definition   158
  example in shooting schedule 137
SPLIT SCREEN
  definition   158
SPOTTING ERRORS
  in capitalization of camera cues 57
  in character introduction   59
  in consistency in character cues 79
  in NOTE: to director, technicians 63
  no capitalization of enters and exits 63
  in (O.S.) vs (O.C.)   65
  in personal direction:
    under character cue   83
    don't end a page with   85
  in scene heading information placed
    stage direction   36B
  in scene numbering   31
  use of AND and THRU
    (omitted scenes in revisions) 113

STAGE DIRECTION
  breaking from one page to
    another   67
  capitalization rules   55, 61, 166
  composite   70
  definitiion   7, 53
  exercises and key   71-73
  format and tabs   53
STOCK SHOTS
  definition   158
  in parentheses   33
  scene headings, example   37d/e
SUBJECTIVE CAMERA
  definition   159
SUPERIMPOSED (SUPER)
  definition   159

- T -

TABS - SUMMARY   161
  Appendix A (see specific heading;
    character cue, etc.)
THREE CAMERA FORMAT
  definition   159
TITLE
  on cover   13-18
  on revised pages   115
  on shooting schedules   135
  on fly/title page   20
  placement on first page, screenplay 21, 22
TITLES
  begin and end   61b
  of books, songs & movies
    capitalized in direction   61d
TIME
  in scene headings   29, 33
TRAVEL DAY
  shooting schedule   138
  example   152
TRAVELING SHOT
  explained   39p
TYPEWRITER
  tabs for filmed format   11
TYPING SCRIPTS PROFESSIONALLY
  checking out the script   10
TWO SHOT
  explained   38

- V -

VOICE OVER (V.O.)
  capitalization in direction 61
  definition   7, 159
(V.O.) and (O.S.)
  in character cues, explained 75
WORD PROCESSING/P.C.'S
  macros   5
  pitch and point explained 4
  tabs and margins suggested 5

- Z -

ZOOM
  example   107